A Compass for your Basic Data Set-up

Preface

I am excited to share the valuable insights I have gained over the past 15 years in data analytics, including a decade of hands-on experience setting up data systems from scratch for renowned e-commerce and media industries. My work in these fields has provided me with a wealth of practical knowledge about creating scalable, reliable data infrastructures, which I am eager to pass on to entrepreneurs and business leaders. For example, during my tenure in the media sector, I led the creation of a comprehensive data infrastructure from the ground up, enabling real-time analytics and improving decision-making across multiple regions. Similarly, in e-commerce, I implemented scalable data solutions that streamlined customer analytics and optimized marketing effectiveness. These experiences have given me unique insights into the challenges and strategies for establishing robust data foundations in startup environments.

The goal of this book is to guide young start-ups in setting up data systems within their organizations by providing practical and actionable insights. This guidance is rooted in real-world examples drawn from my 15 years of experience. This book provides practical, actionable advice for start-ups to effectively manage and utilize data.

There are a lot of learning that I learned the very hard way over my 15 years of experience. I tried to jot all of them down in this book. I believe you should have great benefit by going through this book, as you can learn through my mistakes and don't have to re-invent the same wheel again.

TABLE OF CONTENTS

Introduction

Importance of Data

In today's competitive world, data is the fuel that powers modern startups. With limited time and resources, young companies cannot afford trial-and-error approaches. Instead, they need to make every decision count, and data provides the clarity and confidence to do just that.

Over my 15 years of experience in data analytics, spanning multiple industries like media-streaming, e-commerce, retail, healthcare, and transport, I have seen firsthand how the right data strategy can transform businesses. From leading data architecture and analytics to building end-to-end data infrastructures for big companies, I've helped organizations leverage data to

- Optimize user engagement and retention,
- Drive cost efficiencies, and
- Make faster, more informed decisions.

The role of data in startups is even more pivotal because they operate on tight budgets and high stakes. A well-defined data strategy helps startups identify opportunities, streamline operations, and stay ahead of competitors.

In a data-driven organization, everyone, from the founders to the team members, uses data to guide decisions. A data-driven culture fosters accountability, transparency, and continuous improvement.

Data isn't just numbers on a spreadsheet—it's the story of your business. Start building that story today, and you'll have the clarity and confidence to write the next chapter of your startup's success.

The Challenges Young Companies Face When Handling Data

While the potential of data is immense, startups often struggle to harness it effectively. These challenges are not unique but amplified for young companies operating with limited resources and rapidly evolving goals. Here are the most common hurdles startups face:

1. **Lack of Clear Strategy**: Startups often dive into data collection without a clear understanding of what they aim to achieve. This leads to data overload without actionable insights. Without well-defined goals, efforts become scattered, and the value of data diminishes.

2. **Scattered and Siloed Data**: In early stages, data is often spread across multiple tools, spreadsheets, and systems. This fragmentation makes it challenging to consolidate, analyze, and extract meaningful insights. Teams struggle to align decisions because they lack a single source of truth.

3. **Limited Technical Expertise**: Startups often operate without dedicated data teams. This lack of in-house expertise leads to missed opportunities to identify meaningful patterns, apply effective analytics, or use tools to their full potential.

4. **Choosing the Right Tools**: The sheer number of analytics platforms and tools available today can overwhelm startups. Many companies overspend on complex systems they don't need, while others underinvest and rely on tools that fail to scale as the business grows.

5. **Resource Constraints**: Startups work with limited budgets, time, and personnel. Building a robust data infrastructure often takes a back seat when day-to-day operations demand immediate attention. This leaves startups without the foundational systems needed for long-term success.

6. **Inconsistent Data Practices**: As startups grow, teams often collect and manage data inconsistently. Without defined processes or data governance frameworks, errors multiply, duplicate efforts occur, and trust in the data diminishes over time.

7. **Lack of Actionable Insights**: Collecting data is only half the battle. Many startups struggle to turn raw data into insights that drive decision-making. Without a clear framework for analysis, startups risk getting stuck in a cycle of collecting numbers without extracting value.

These challenges may seem daunting, but they can be addressed with the right approach—one that balances simplicity, scalability, and impact.

Common Mistakes Startups Make with Data

Startups often face challenges in effectively managing and leveraging data. While the potential of data-driven decision-making is immense, there are common mistakes that can derail progress or lead to suboptimal results. Below are the pitfalls and actionable recommendations to help startups avoid them.

1. Collecting Right Amount of Data with Clear Goals

- **Mistake**: Startups often fall into two extremes when it comes to data collection:
  - Over-Collecting Irrelevant Data**:** Attempting to collect every possible piece of data without defining clear goals.
  - Under-Collecting Necessary Data**:** Prioritizing rapid feature development and release over measuring their effectiveness.
- **Impact**: Leads to unreliable insights and incorrect decisions.
  - Over-Collecting**:** Overwhelms teams with irrelevant data, complicates analysis, and leads to inaction.
  - Under-Collecting**:** Leaves teams without insights into how features perform, whether drive value or need improvement.
- **Solution**:
  - Define Clear Objectives**:**
    - Before collecting any data or developing features, identify the specific goals you aim to achieve (e.g., "Track user churn rates" or "Analyze marketing ROI").
    - Ensure these goals align with business KPIs.
  - Tie Data Collection to Feature Development**:**
    - Every feature should have measurable success criteria. For example, "Track adoption rate of Feature X within first 30 days" or "Determine impact of Feature Y on user retention."
  - Integrate Analytics from the Start**:**
    - Build data tracking mechanisms during the development process (e.g., user behavior tracking, A/B testing).

        - Even lightweight analytics can provide valuable insights.
    - Act on Insights:
        - Regularly review data to evaluate feature objectives.
        - Use insights to iterate, pivot, or discontinue features as necessary.

2. Ignoring Data Quality

- **Mistake**: Using inaccurate, incomplete, or inconsistent data for decision-making.
- **Impact**: Leads to unreliable insights and incorrect decisions.
- **Solution**:
    - Implement data validation processes to check for errors, duplicates, and inconsistencies.
    - Regularly clean and audit your data pipelines.
    - Use tools like Great Expectations for automated data quality checks.

3. Failing to Build a Scalable Data Infrastructure

- **Mistake**: Using tools or systems that cannot handle increasing data volume as the startup grows.
- **Impact**: Creates bottlenecks and requires costly overhauls later.
- **Solution**:
    - Start with scalable, cloud-based solutions like BigQuery, Snowflake, or Databricks.
    - Regularly review your infrastructure for potential scalability issues.

4. Overcomplicating the Technology Stack

- **Mistake**: Adopting too many tools or technologies without proper integration or expertise.
- **Impact**: Leads to inefficiencies, increased costs, and team frustration.
- **Solution**:
  - Focus on tools that align with your current needs and can scale as your business grows.
  - Limit your stack to essential components, ensuring seamless integration.

5. Neglecting Data Governance

- **Mistake**: Ignoring data privacy regulations and governance practices.
- **Impact**: Increases risk of data breaches, non-compliance fines, and reputational damage.
- **Solution**:
  - Establish data governance policies early, including role-based access controls.
  - Stay updated on regulations like GDPR, CCPA, and HIPAA.
  - Use encryption and anonymization for sensitive data.

6. Underutilizing Analytics Tools

- **Mistake**: Investing in advanced analytics tools but failing to fully leverage their capabilities.
- **Impact**: Results in wasted resources and underwhelming insights.
- **Solution**:
  - Train teams on how to use tools like Tableau, Power BI, or Looker effectively.
  - Start with basic features and gradually explore advanced functionalities like predictive analytics.

7. Delaying Investment in Data Teams

- **Mistake**: Postponing the hiring of data professionals until operations become overwhelming.
- **Impact**: Slows down the ability to derive insights and make informed decisions.
- **Solution**:
  - Hire a part-time data consultant or freelance data engineer in the early stages.
  - Gradually build an in-house team as data needs grow.

8. Not Establishing Clear Ownership of Data

- **Mistake**: Lack of clarity on who is responsible for managing and analyzing data.
- **Impact**: Leads to mismanagement, duplicated efforts, and accountability gaps.
- **Solution**:
  - Define roles and responsibilities for data collection, processing, and analysis.
  - Assign a data owner or data steward to oversee governance and quality.

9. Ignoring Real-Time Data Opportunities

- **Mistake**: Focusing only on batch processing while ignoring the benefits of real-time analytics.
- **Impact**: Misses opportunities for immediate action, such as responding to user behavior or market trends.
- **Solution**:
  - Use real-time data platforms like Kafka, Google Pub/Sub, or AWS Kinesis for time-sensitive use cases.
  - Balance batch and real-time analytics based on your business needs.

10. Failing to Communicate Insights Effectively

- **Mistake**: Presenting data in overly complex or poorly designed formats that stakeholders cannot understand.
- **Impact**: Reduces the impact of insights and hinders decision-making.
- **Solution**:
  - Create dashboards that are clear, visually appealing, and tailored to the audience.
  - Use storytelling techniques to make data insights more relatable and actionable.

Avoiding these common mistakes can significantly enhance a startup's ability to harness the power of data. By focusing on data quality, scalability, governance, and communication, startups can establish a strong foundation for growth and innovation.

Overview of the Book's Approach and Benefits

This book is born from my personal experiences helping organizations, both large and small, unlock the power of their data. It is designed specifically for startup founders, managers, and teams looking to take the first steps toward becoming data-driven businesses.

Here's what makes this guide unique:

- **Non-Conventional Approaches:** Innovative methodologies like ELT (Extract, Load, Transform), which prioritize efficiency and scalability in modern data pipelines, ensuring you stay ahead of traditional practices.
- **Practical Solutions**: Step-by-step frameworks to set up your data strategy, from collection to insights, even with limited budgets.
- **Real-World Experience**: Lessons drawn from my work with global giants and fast-growing startups, where I helped design scalable data systems and actionable analytics solutions.
- **Actionable Insights**: Clear guidance on choosing the right tools, defining the right metrics, and implementing best practices for data governance and analysis.

With credentials that include speaking at six industry conferences on data analytics and earning accolades for driving impactful, data-backed results, I bring not only technical expertise but also an understanding of the unique challenges startups face.

Drawing from real-world methodologies I've developed over 15 years, including setting up scalable data infrastructures for renowned media and e-commerce companies. These strategies helped improve operational efficiency, reduce customer churn, and enable informed decision-making.

By the end of this book, you will:

- Understand how to organize and analyze your data,
- Learn to make decisions that drive business growth, and
- Build a data foundation that scales as your startup grows.

Let's embark on this journey to transform your startup into a **data-driven powerhouse**. With the right mindset and tools, you'll find that data isn't just for large corporations—it's a startup's greatest asset.

Part I: Basic Data-Setup

"You can't improve what you don't measure."
– *Peter Drucker*, Management Consultant and Author

In Part I: Basic Data-Setup, we lay a practical and structured foundation for your startup's data journey. This section is your guide to setting up an organized, reliable, and scalable data infrastructure that will empower you to make better business decisions, even if you're starting from scratch.

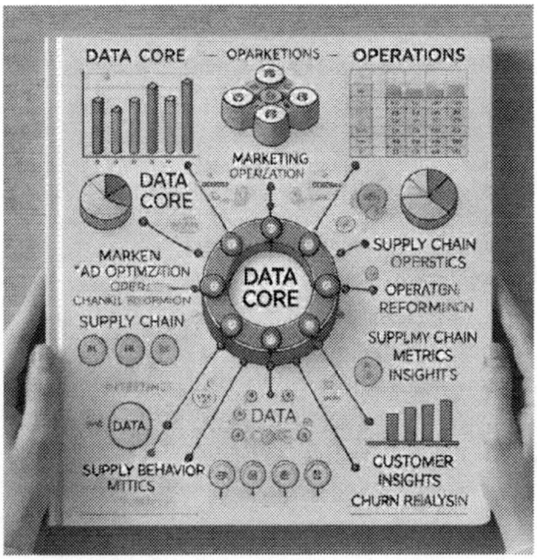

For example, data collected from marketing campaigns can help optimize ad spending and identify effective channels. In operations, data on supply chain metrics can streamline processes and reduce costs. For customer retention, analyzing user behavior and feedback provides actionable insights to improve engagement and reduce churn. This interconnected system ensures that every department benefits from a unified, data-driven strategy, driving overall growth and efficiency.

What to Expect in Part I:

- Part I begins with an exploration of the significance of data for startups, guiding you in defining **clear data goals** to prevent information overload and maintain focus on actionable insights.
- You will learn how to build **data pipelines** that collect, transform, and centralize data from various sources without requiring heavy technical expertise.
- We'll cover the importance of **data warehousing** and guide you through choosing tools like **BigQuery, Databricks, Snowflake, or Redshift** to store and manage your data effectively.
- You will discover how to turn raw data into meaningful insights through **dashboards and reporting**, using tools like Tableau, Power BI, or Looker.
- Finally, you'll be introduced to basic **data analytics**, enabling you to analyze trends, measure KPIs, and make decisions that drive growth.

What You Will Achieve by the End of Part I:

By the time you complete Part I, you will:

- Have a **solid data foundation** for your startup—organized, clean, and reliable.
- Know how to set up and automate **data pipelines** and **warehousing** systems.
- Build **dashboards** that give you real-time insights into your key business metrics.
- Understand **basic analytics** to measure performance, identify opportunities, and troubleshoot challenges effectively.
- Be equipped with cost-effective tools and frameworks that can scale as your startup grows.

Part I will empower you to **transform raw data into actionable insights**, enabling you to make smarter decisions, align your teams, and grow your startup with confidence. This foundational setup is critical for success and will prepare you for the advanced data set-up.

Chapter One: Building the Foundation

Chapter One: Building the Foundation

This is the most important step of Data-setup, because if the base of the building is weak then the whole building is likely to crumble. So you need to think very wisely and leave no stones unturned while setting up the foundation of the data.

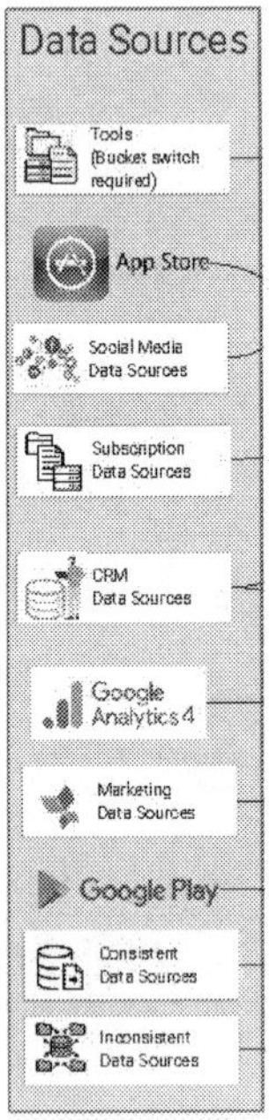

1.1 Importance of Data for Startups

Data is more than just a collection of numbers—it's the foundation on which informed decisions are made. For startups, which often operate with limited resources, data becomes a crucial asset that can differentiate between success and failure. The role of data in a startup's success lies in its ability to provide insights into business performance, customer behavior, and market trends.

Key Benefits of Data in Startups:

- **Informed Decision-Making**: Data helps startup founders move away from gut-based decision-making to making evidence-backed choices. For example, by analyzing customer feedback and purchase behavior, you can decide which features or products to prioritize without guessing.
- **Identifying Opportunities and Risks**: By monitoring key metrics (like customer retention rates, sales growth, or website traffic), startups can spot emerging trends, new market opportunities, or areas where things may be going off track, allowing them to act quickly.
- **Cost Efficiency**: Data helps startups optimize operations by enabling resource allocation to the most effective channels, reducing wasted spend, and improving ROI. However, it's equally important to manage the costs of data collection and analysis. Implementing FinOps practices and tracking metrics like *Cost Per Subscriber (CPS)* ensures that data-driven decisions remain cost-efficient. By aligning data strategies with business goals and sharing cost metrics internally, startups can balance operational impact with financial sustainability.
- **Scalability**: As startups grow, data becomes essential in tracking the scalability of business processes. For example, understanding your operational bottlenecks through data analysis helps you streamline operations as your team or customer base expands.

1.2 Defining Data Goals

Before diving into the data collection process, it's essential to define clear, specific goals. What do you want to know, and how will this information help you grow your business? Establishing data goals allows you to focus on collecting relevant, actionable data that drives your business forward.

How to Define Data Goals:

- **Understand Your Business Needs**: Every startup is unique, so the questions you need to answer will depend on your business model. For example, if you run an e-commerce business, understanding conversion rates (the percentage of visitors who make a purchase) is critical. If you offer a subscription-based service, customer churn rate (the rate at which customers leave) might be your key metric.
- **Align with Business Objectives**: Your data goals should be aligned with your broader business objectives. If your goal is to expand your market reach, you may want to focus on data that tracks customer acquisition and retention. If you're aiming to improve product features, gathering data on user experience and satisfaction becomes essential.
- **Prioritize Key Metrics (KPIs)**: Once you have a clear goal, it’s time to define your key performance indicators (KPIs)—the metrics that will guide your decisions.

Examples of goal-oriented questions:

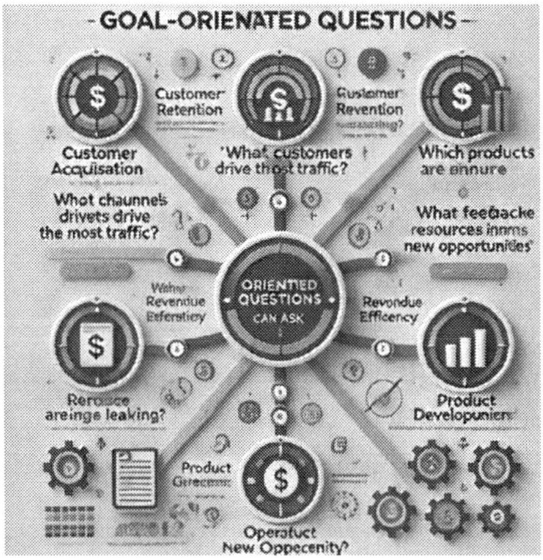

Customer Acquisition

- How are users finding my product or service?
- What channels drive the most traffic?
- What is the conversion rate for each acquisition channel?
- How much does it cost to acquire a new customer (Customer Acquisition Cost - CAC)?

Customer Retention

- Why are users leaving my product or service?
- What features or experiences increase user engagement?
- What is the lifetime value (LTV) of my customers, and how can it be improved?
- How effective are loyalty programs or re-engagement strategies?

Revenue Growth

- Which products or services generate highest profit margins?
- What customer segments are the most profitable?
- How effective are upselling and cross-selling strategies?
- How does demand impact revenue and how can be optimized?

Operational Efficiency

- Where are resources being wasted in my processes?
- How can my workflows or operations be streamlined?
- Are there tools or automations that can reduce manual work?
- What bottlenecks impact my supply chain or delivery systems?

Product Development

- Which product features are used the most, and why?
- What customer pain points need to be addressed?
- What feedback or trends indicate the need for new product development?
- Are there opportunities for product innovation based on user behavior?

Market Insights

- How does my business compare to competitors?
- What trends or opportunities exist in my target market?
- Are there untapped demographics or regions worth exploring?
- What industry shifts or customer preferences could affect my growth?

1.3 Tools for Collecting, Organizing, and Visualizing Data

Selecting tools is the first step in any data-driven strategy. Startups often rely on multiple tools to gather data from various sources, such as customer interactions, website visits, social media, and more. The tools you choose for data collection, organisation and visualization play a crucial role in ensuring that your data is useful and actionable. Selecting the right set of tools can streamline the process, save time, and reduce errors.

Data Collection Tools

Data collection is the foundation of any data strategy. Startups can use these tools to gather actionable data from various sources:

1. **Google Analytics**
   - Tracks website traffic, user demographics, and behavior.
   - Provides insights into visitor flow, enabling you to optimize landing pages and user journeys.
   - Essential for identifying high-performing content or pages with high drop-off rates.

2. **Appsflyer or Firebase**

    - Designed for mobile app analytics.
    - Tracks in-app events, user retention, and install sources.
    - Firebase also offers additional features like push notifications and crash reporting.

3. **CRM Platforms (Braze, Salesforce, HubSpot, Zoho)**

    - These systems collect customer interaction data, such as purchase history, email engagement, and customer service interactions.
    - Allows you to manage relationships, personalize outreach, and analyze sales pipelines.
    - Salesforce and HubSpot, for example, provide advanced analytics and integrations for scaling startups.

4. **Social Media Analytics (Facebook Insights, Twitter Analytics, Google Trends)**

    - Track engagement metrics, audience demographics, and sentiment across platforms.
    - Helps you refine your social media strategy by identifying what content resonates with your audience.
    - Google Trends offers insights into popular search topics, helping align your content with trending subjects.

5. **Google Forms or Typeform**

    - Cost-effective tools for collecting direct feedback from customers, employees, or partners.
    - Ideal for surveys, customer satisfaction scores, and gathering qualitative data.

Data Organization Tools

Organizing data ensures that it is clean, accessible, and easy to analyze. These tools are suitable for startups at different stages:

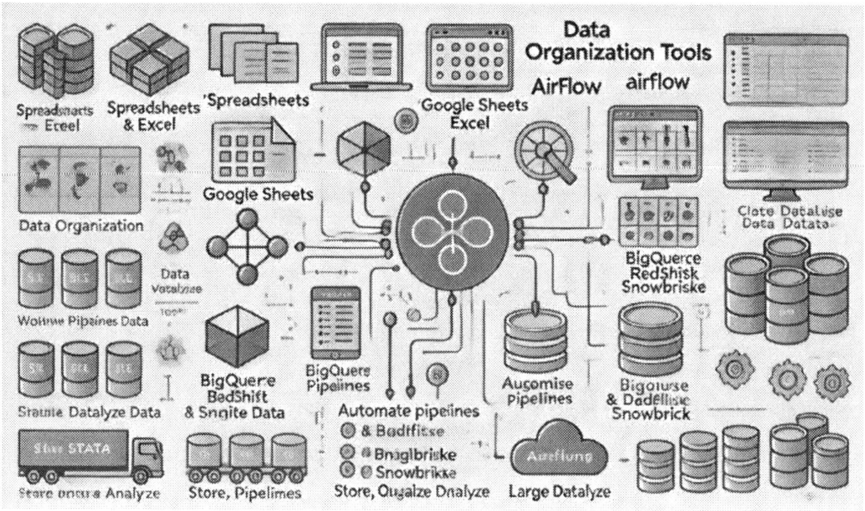

1. **Spreadsheets (Google Sheets, Excel)**
   - Perfect for startups in the early stages with smaller datasets.
   - Enables simple calculations, sorting, and basic data visualization.
   - Excel's advanced functions like PivotTables and macros can support more complex data management tasks.

2. **Pipelines (Airflow)**
   - A workflow orchestration tool to migrate data seamlessly between sources and warehouses.
   - Automates data pipelines, ensuring data flows consistently without manual intervention.

3. **Warehousing (BigQuery, Redshift, Snowflake, Databricks)**
   - These cloud-based platforms allow you to store and query large datasets efficiently.
   - Snowflake excels in scalability and easy collaboration, while BigQuery integrates seamlessly with Google tools.
   - Databricks offers machine learning capabilities in addition to data storage.

4. **Airtable**
   - Combines the simplicity of spreadsheets with the power of relational databases.
   - Useful for organizing project data, product inventories, or customer feedback.
   - Provides customizable templates and integrations to streamline workflows.

Data Visualization Tools

Once data is collected and organized, visualization tools bring it to life. They help you identify patterns, trends, and anomalies with ease.

With the organized dashboards it is easy visualize actionable insights:

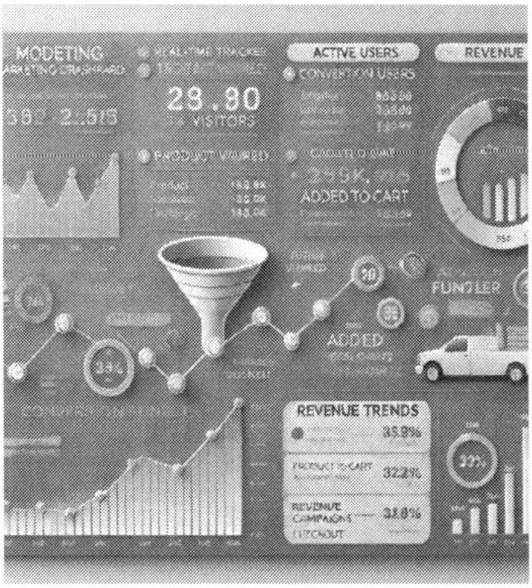

Example: A marketing dashboard designed for an e-commerce startup includes key metrics like website traffic, conversion rates, and revenue per campaign. The top section displays a real-time traffic tracker, while the middle section highlights conversion funnels with drop-off points clearly marked. At the bottom, revenue trends are visualized with filters for specific campaigns.

1. **Basic (Google Sheets, Excel)**
   - Ideal for creating quick charts and graphs for smaller datasets.
   - Simple tools for presenting data to internal teams or stakeholders without extensive preparation.

2. **Advanced (Looker, Tableau, Power BI)**
   - **Looker**: Offers deep integrations with databases and a highly customizable visualization interface.
   - **Tableau**: Excels at creating interactive, dynamic dashboards with drag-and-drop functionality.
   - **Power BI**: Provides cost-effective solutions for startups looking for powerful analytics combined with Microsoft Office integrations.

To assist readers in selecting the most suitable visualization tool, here is a comparison of these platforms based on key features:

Feature	**Tableau**	**Looker**	**Power BI**	**Open-Source Options**
Ease of Use	Intuitive drag-and-drop interface.	Requires SQL knowledge for custom queries.	User-friendly, especially for Microsoft ecosystem users.	Varies; some require technical expertise (e.g., D3.js, Apache Superset).
Pricing	Per-user subscription; can be costly for small teams	Subscription-based; higher initial investment	Affordable with free desktop version and tiered pricing.	Typically free; costs may arise for customization.
Integration	Integrates with multiple data sources, including cloud platforms.	Seamless integration with Google Cloud and APIs.	Best for Microsoft products and Excel users.	Integration depends on the specific tool.
Scalability	Suitable for teams of all sizes; handles large datasets well.	Scalable, ideal for enterprise-level applications.	Works well for small to medium-sized businesses.	Depends on the tool; may require additional development for scaling.
Visualization	Offers rich, interactive visuals with extensive customization.	Focused on embedding analytics into workflows.	Provides robust, customizable visuals; less flexible than Tableau.	High flexibility; requires manual coding for advanced visuals.

This comparison can help readers evaluate which tool aligns with their business needs, technical expertise, and budget constraints.

By leveraging these tools, startups can transform raw data into actionable insights without overwhelming their budgets or teams. The right tools simplify processes, automate repetitive tasks, and ensure data accuracy, leaving founders more time to focus on scaling their business.

1.4 Framework for Collecting and Organizing Data

Define data lifecycle framework: break down the journey of data into clear stages, ensuring startups can move seamlessly from raw data to meaningful decisions.

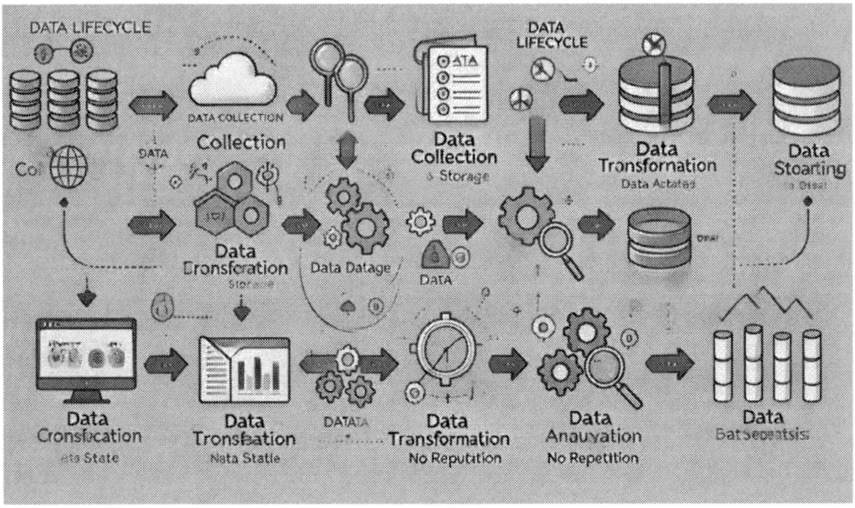

1. Data Collection

This is starting point where data is gathered from various sources.

- **Sources of Data**:
  - **Web and Mobile Analytics**: Tools like Google Analytics, Firebase, and Appsflyer track user activity.
  - **Customer Data**: CRM platforms like Braze, HubSpot and Salesforce capture customer interactions.
  - **Operational Data**: IoT devices, log files, or ERP systems provide insights into business processes.
  - **Surveys and Feedback**: Google Forms or Typeform allow direct data collection from customers and employees.
- **Best Practice**: Focus on collecting only relevant data that aligns with your business goals to avoid information overload.
- **Example**: An e-commerce startup collects data on user clicks, purchase history, and abandoned carts to identify high-converting product categories.

2. Data Storage

Once data is collected, it must be stored securely and efficiently to allow easy access.

- **Types of Storage Solutions**:
  - **Spreadsheets**: Google Sheets or Excel for smaller datasets.
  - **Databases**: MySQL, PostgreSQL for structured data storage.
  - **Cloud-Based Warehousing**: Platforms like BigQuery, Redshift, Snowflake, or Databricks for large-scale, fast querying.
- **Best Practice**: Ensure data is centralized to prevent silos across teams. Adopt cloud-based tools for scalability and flexibility.
- **Example**: A media company stores terabytes of streaming data in Databricks/BigQuery/Snowflake to allow real-time querying for content recommendations.

3. Data Cleaning

Raw data is rarely ready for analysis. Cleaning ensures that data is accurate, consistent, and usable.

- **Tasks Involved**:
  - Removing duplicates and incomplete entries.
  - Correcting errors like misspellings or incorrect formats.
  - Standardizing naming conventions (e.g., product categories).
- **Tools**: Data cleaning tools like **OpenRefine**, Python libraries (e.g., Pandas), and built-in features in Excel or Google Sheets.
- **Best Practice**: Automate cleaning processes where possible to save time and reduce human error.
- **Example**: An early-stage fintech startup cleans transaction logs to remove duplicate entries, ensuring accurate financial reporting.

4. Data Transformation

Data often needs to be transformed into formats suitable for analysis.

- **Key Processes**:
  - Aggregation: Summarizing data (e.g., monthly revenue totals).
  - Categorization: Grouping data (e.g., high-, medium-, low-performing products).
  - Merging: Combining datasets from multiple sources into a single, unified format.
- **Tools**: Workflow orchestration tools like Apache Airflow or ETL pipelines automate transformation processes.
- **Best Practice**: Build flexible pipelines that allow you to add new transformations as the business scales.
- **Example**: An e-commerce company aggregates daily order data by region to identify which locations contribute the most sales.

5. Data Analysis

This stage is where patterns, trends, and insights are uncovered to inform decision-making.

- **Types of Analysis**:
  - **Descriptive Analytics**: What happened? (e.g., monthly sales trends).
  - **Diagnostic Analytics**: Why did it happen? (e.g., high churn in a specific product line).
  - **Predictive Analytics**: What will happen? (e.g., forecasting future demand).
- **Tools**: Use tools like **Power BI**, **Tableau**, or Python libraries like Matplotlib and Scikit-Learn for advanced analysis.
- **Best Practice**: Always align analysis with your business goals—focus on KPIs and metrics that drive growth.
- **Example**: A SaaS startup analyzes churn trends and identifies that customers are leaving due to a lack of onboarding support.

6. Data Reporting/Visualization

The final step is to present data in a clear and actionable format to stakeholders.

- **Common Reporting Tools**:
  - **Dashboards**: Tools like Tableau, Power BI, or Looker for real-time visualization.
  - **Static Reports**: Excel or Google Sheets for periodic reporting.
  - **Automated Reports**: Scheduling tools that distribute insights daily, weekly, or monthly.
- **Best Practice**: Use visuals (charts, graphs, funnels) to highlight key takeaways and simplify complex data.
- **Example**: A startup presents a weekly performance dashboard to track website traffic, user conversions, and marketing ROI.

Summary: The Data Lifecycle Framework

1. **Data Collection**: Gather data from relevant sources.
2. **Data Storage**: Store data securely and accessibly.
3. **Data Cleaning**: Remove errors and inconsistencies.
4. **Data Transformation**: Prepare data for analysis through aggregation or categorization.
5. **Data Analysis**: Extract insights to inform business decisions.
6. **Data Reporting/Visualization**: Present findings clearly using dashboards or reports.

1.5 Case Study: A Startup That Leveraged Data Early

Let's dive into the story of NikShop, a fictional yet realistic example of an early-stage e-commerce startup that successfully used data to drive growth.

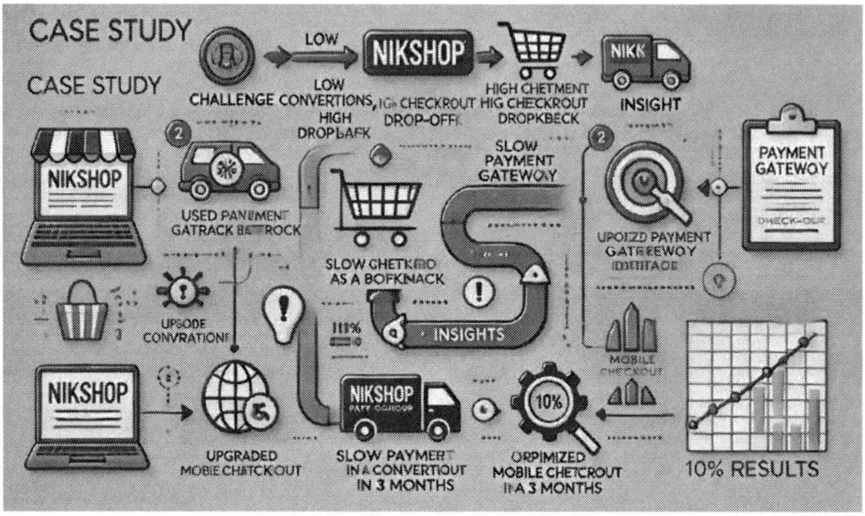

The Challenge:

When NikShop launched, the team noticed a mismatch between their website traffic and actual sales conversions. While marketing campaigns drove a healthy number of visitors to the platform, the **conversion rate remained stubbornly low**, and visitors were abandoning their carts at the final step.

The Approach:

To diagnose the issue, the founders adopted a **data-driven approach**:

1. **Tracking User Behavior**: Using **Google Analytics**, they mapped the customer journey to identify bottlenecks.
   - They monitored user flow from homepage to product pages, all the way to the checkout.

2. **Pinpointing Drop-Off Points**: Data revealed that a significant portion of users dropped off during the **payment process**.
   - This key insight raised a red flag about the **payment gateway experience**.

The Insight:

Upon further investigation, the NikShop team discovered two specific issues:

1. The **payment gateway** was slow, leading to user frustration.
2. Mobile users faced frequent errors during payment processing.

These technical shortcomings discouraged users from completing their purchases, impacting revenue.

The Solution:

With actionable insights from their analysis, NikShop implemented the following changes:

- **Upgraded the Payment Gateway**: They switched to a faster, more reliable gateway with a smoother mobile experience.
- **Improved Mobile Optimization**: They ensured the checkout flow was responsive and tested for errors across all devices.
- **Introduced Guest Checkout**: To reduce friction, they allowed users to check out without mandatory account creation.

The Results:

Within **three months** of making these changes:

- Conversion rates increased by **10%**.
- Customer satisfaction scores improved significantly, especially among mobile users.
- The revenue from repeat customers grew as users returned for a smoother experience.

Key Takeaway for Startups:
The NikShop story demonstrates how even **basic data collection and analysis**—like tracking user journeys and identifying drop-off points—can uncover critical insights. By acting on this data, startups can:

- Solve immediate bottlenecks.
- Enhance the user experience.
- Drive measurable improvements in conversions and business growth.

For startups, the lesson is clear: Embracing a **data-driven mindset** early on can unlock powerful opportunities to optimize operations and improve customer outcomes.

1.6 Action Plan: Setting Up Your Data Foundation

This action plan is the critical first step toward building a strong and scalable data-driven strategy for your startup. By following these steps, you'll create a solid foundation that empowers you to make smarter, faster, and more impactful decisions—paving the way for sustained growth and success.

By the end of this chapter, you should have a roadmap for building your startup's data foundation. Here's an actionable plan:

1. Define Your Key Questions: Identify the top 3-5 questions you need answers to. For example:

- E-commerce Startups: Questions might include, "What is our conversion rate from visitors to customers?" or "Which product categories generate the most revenue?"
- SaaS Startups: Common questions could be, "What is our monthly churn rate?" or "Which features are driving the most engagement among users?"
- Marketplace Startups: Questions might include, "How many buyers and sellers are active on our platform weekly?" or "What's the average transaction value across different categories?"

By tailoring your questions to your business model, you ensure that the data you collect directly supports your startup's growth and decision-making processes.

2. Choose Simple Tools: Select tools that fit your current needs and budget. Start small and scale later. For example:

- Google Sheets: A simple and cost-effective tool for tracking and organizing data in the early stages.
- Google Analytics: Essential for tracking website performance and user behavior.
- HubSpot CRM: A free and scalable option for managing customer relationships and sales pipelines.
- Firebase: Perfect for startups focusing on mobile app analytics and in-app event tracking.

By starting with these tools, you can address your immediate data needs while leaving room for more advanced systems as your startup grows.

3. Track the Right Metrics: Focus on a few key performance indicators (KPIs) relevant to your business goals.

4. Centralize Your Data: Create a single source of truth by consolidating data into one system or tool. For example:

- *Airtable*: A versatile tool that combines the simplicity of spreadsheets with the power of relational databases, making it ideal for organizing and managing diverse datasets.
- *BigQuery*: A cloud-based data warehouse that allows you to store and query large datasets quickly and efficiently, perfect for startups looking to scale.
- *Snowflake*: Known for its scalability and collaboration features, it's an excellent option for creating a centralized data repository.

Centralizing your data ensures consistency, reduces redundancy, and allows for faster and more accurate analysis.

5. Regularly Review Data: Set a cadence (e.g., daily or weekly) to review data trends and insights. During these review sessions, focus on:

- *Performance Metrics*: Analyze KPIs relevant to your business, such as sales growth, customer acquisition costs, or churn rates.
- *Data Quality*: Check for inconsistencies, missing entries, or outdated data that might affect decision-making.
- *Emerging Trends*: Identify patterns or shifts in customer behavior, market demands, or operational bottlenecks.
- *Actionable Insights*: Translate your findings into clear action points. For example, if user engagement on a specific feature is declining, plan a targeted campaign or prioritize feature updates.
- *Collaboration*: Use these sessions to involve your team, ensuring that insights are shared and integrated into strategic planning.

1.7 Conclusion: Building a Strong Data Foundation

The foundation of a successful startup relies heavily on data. By understanding the role of data, setting clear goals, selecting the right tools, and creating a culture that embraces data, you're positioning your business for long-term success.

Building a data foundation might seem daunting, but it's one of the most rewarding investments you can make for your startup. Data enables you to make smarter decisions, grow faster, and operate more efficiently. Remember, the sooner you start leveraging data effectively, the greater your chances of outpacing your competition.

In this chapter, we've covered the first steps to setting up your data foundation—from defining your goals to choosing tools and frameworks that fit your startup's needs. You now have the basics to start organizing your data and turning it into actionable insights.

If you have thoroughly completed this chapter and solidified the fundamentals, then you've covered the most critical part of your data journey. The rest of the chapters will build upon the decisions you've made here. I recommend taking a moment to step back and reflect: **Are you confident in the choices you've made so far?** In the upcoming chapters, we will focus on implementing the tools and technologies you've selected.

My Recommendation based on my Experience in Data Stream: Try to avoid moving your data across multiple cloud platforms. Instead, aim to maintain your data pipelines, warehouses, and visualization tools within a single cloud ecosystem. This will help eliminate cloud latency issues. If your dashboards take more than a minute to load, no one will use them. In today's fast-paced world, attention spans are incredibly short, and if you lose your audience's attention, it's nearly impossible to get it back.

In the next chapter, we'll dive deeper into building data pipelines, where you'll learn how to streamline data flow, ensure accuracy, and create a system that scales as your startup grows. Let's keep building!

Chapter Two:
Building
Data Pipelines

Chapter Two: Building Data Pipelines

After selecting the tools for your data strategy, the next critical step is to set up a system that collects, processes, and delivers data to your data warehouse. This step ensures that your data is structured, accessible, and ready for analysis.

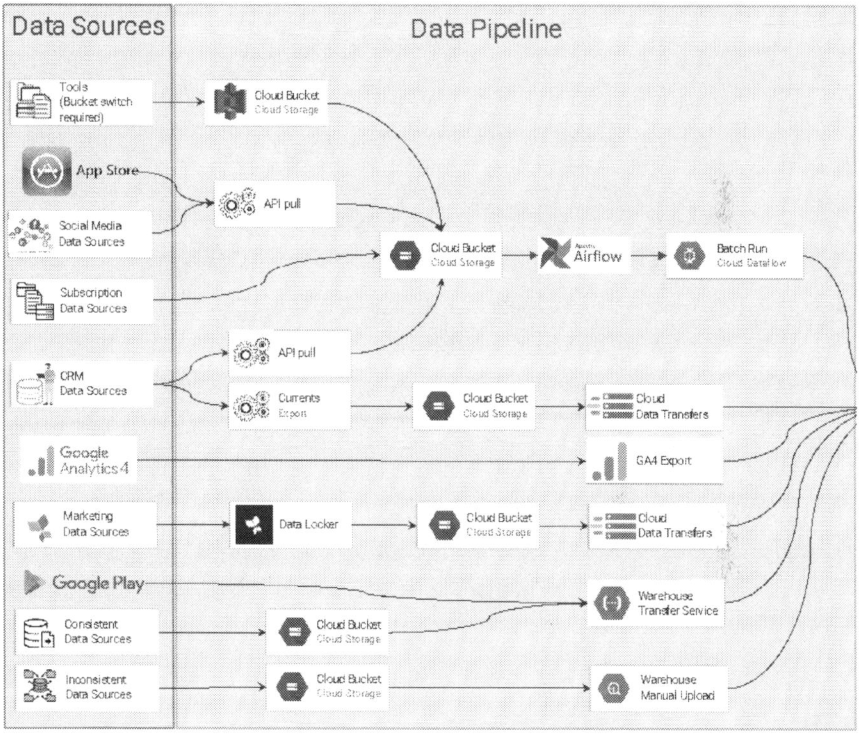

2.1 Defining a Data Pipeline

In today's data-driven landscape, constructing robust data pipelines is crucial for start-ups aiming to leverage insights effectively. Think of data pipelines as the nervous system of your organisation, ensuring that data flows seamlessly from its raw state to insightful information.

A **data pipeline** is a structured series of processes designed to move data from its source to its final destination in a way that ensures it is clean, reliable, and ready for analysis. It acts as the backbone of a data-driven organization, automating the flow of information to eliminate manual handling and reduce errors.

Choosing Between Python Scripts and No-Code Tools

While setting data pipes requires programming knowledge—Python being the most commonly used language—there are numerous no-code tools available in the market that can simplify the process for those without a technical background.

Option 1: Using Python Scripts

- Ideal for startups with tight budgets or strict data privacy concerns.
- Provides flexibility for custom workflows and full control over data processes.
- Can be automated using AWS Lambda, Google Cloud Scheduler, or cron jobs.

Option 2: Leveraging No-Code Tools

- Simplifies the process for non-technical teams.
- Tools like **Fivetran**, **Hevo Data**, **Zapier, Alooma and Stitch Data** provide pre-built connectors and intuitive interfaces.
- Enables quick deployment without the need for programming expertise.

Table for Comparison:

Criteria	*Python Scripts*	*No-Code Tools*
Cost	Low (pay only for cloud hosting)	Subscription fees (varies by tool)
Ease of Use	Requires programming knowledge	User-friendly, no technical skills required
Flexibility	Highly customizable	Limited to tool's capabilities
Scalability	Fully scalable with effort	Scales seamlessly

2.2 Key Components of a Data Pipeline

2.2.1 Data Sources

Capturing data from a diverse range of sources ensures a holistic understanding of your business and user behavior. Here are the few different sources for origin of raw data used in the pipeline:

Websites:

- Tools like **Google Analytics** can track user behavior, including page views, click paths, and session durations.
- Use Case: Optimizing landing pages or identifying high drop-off rates in e-commerce checkouts.

Applications:

- Data from platforms like **Firebase** or **Appsflyer** provides insights into app usage, installs, and crashes.
- Use Case: Tracking user retention and performance metrics for mobile apps.

App Hosting Platforms:

- Sources like the **Apple App Store** or **Google Play Console** can provide download statistics, crash reports, and app performance insights.
- Use Case: Analyzing app growth trends and identifying performance issues.

Subscription Platforms:

- Inhouse. Subscription platform or 3rd parties provide payment data, subscription renewals, and subscribers data.
- Use Case: A logistics startup pulls payment, order and shipment details for delivery tracking.

APIs:

- Third-party APIs (e.g., CRM tools like Salesforce or social media platforms) can provide structured data directly into the pipeline.
- Use Case: Importing Facebook ad performance data for campaign optimization

2.2.2 Data Collection

Data collection is the first stage of any data pipeline and involves extracting raw data from various sources to feed into the pipeline. This step ensures that all relevant data is captured and ready for processing. Depending on the business requirements, data can be collected in real-time or in batches.

Approaches to Data Collection:

1. *Batch Processing*
   - **Definition**: Data is collected and processed at specific intervals, such as hourly, daily, or weekly.
   - **Use Case**: Suitable for scenarios where real-time data isn't required, like generating daily sales reports or consolidating transaction logs.
   - **Example**: A retail startup collects all point-of-sale data from physical stores at the end of the day.

2. *Streaming/Real-Time Processing*
   - **Definition**: Data is collected and processed as it is generated, allowing for immediate insights.
   - **Use Case**: Ideal for businesses that require live data, such as monitoring user activity on a website or tracking IoT device performance.
   - **Example**: A mobile gaming company monitors player engagement metrics in real-time to optimize in-game ads dynamically.

Tools:

- **No-Code Tools**: Fivetran, Stitch Data, or Zapier for automated data extraction.
- **Custom Code**: Python scripts using libraries like `requests` for API calls or `pandas` for reading database outputs.

Best Practices for Data Collection

To ensure your data pipeline is efficient, accurate, and scalable, adopting these best practices is crucial. Proper data collection not only saves time but also prevents issues later in the pipeline, such as data redundancy or quality problems.

1. Prioritize Relevant Data

Collecting unnecessary data can result in bloated storage, higher costs, and confusion during analysis. Focusing only on relevant data ensures that your resources are spent on insights that drive business growth.

How to Do It:

- Define the specific goals and key performance indicators (KPIs) your business wants to track (e.g., conversion rates, churn rates).
- Conduct stakeholder interviews to understand the data needs of various teams (e.g., marketing, operations, finance).
- Avoid over-collecting data that isn't actionable or aligned with your goals.

Example: A SaaS startup prioritizes collecting data on user logins, session durations, and subscription cancellations to monitor user engagement and retention, ignoring less critical metrics like minor feature usage.

2. Ensure Data Quality at the Source

Poor-quality data (e.g., duplicates, incomplete entries, or inconsistent formats) can propagate throughout the pipeline, leading to inaccurate analysis and decision-making.

How to Do It:
- Implement validation checks during data ingestion to ensure completeness and consistency.
- Use tools like **Apache Airflow** to add data validation layers in the pipeline.
- Standardize data formats and naming conventions at the collection stage (e.g., consistent date formats, unit measurements).

Example: A retail startup standardizes product names and categories at the data source to prevent mismatches when analyzing inventory and sales trends.

3. Secure Sensitive Data

Data breaches can harm your business reputation and violate regulations like GDPR or CCPA. Ensuring secure collection and storage of sensitive information (e.g., payment details, personal data) is essential.

How to Do It:
- Encrypt sensitive data at rest and in transit using secure protocols (e.g., HTTPS, TLS).
- Limit access to sensitive data through role-based permissions.
- Use tokenization for payment data and anonymize personal identifiers where possible.

Example: A subscription-based business encrypts payment data collected from Stripe and restricts access to only authorized team members.

4. Maintain a Consistent Schedule

Regular data collection ensures continuity, preventing gaps in datasets that can lead to inaccurate insights.

How to Do It:

- Schedule batch data collection processes (e.g., hourly or daily intervals) using tools like **Apache Airflow** or **cron jobs**.
- For real-time data needs, use event streaming platforms like **Kafka** or **Kinesis** to ingest data continuously.
- Ensure time zones are synchronized across sources to prevent inconsistencies.

Example: An e-commerce company collects sales data every hour, ensuring timely updates to their inventory dashboard.

5. Use Scalable Tools for Data Collection

As your business grows, your data volume and variety will increase. Tools that can scale effortlessly prevent pipeline bottlenecks and allow for seamless expansion.

How to Do It:

- Start with cloud-native tools like for Python (Google Cloud Scheduler/Google Cloud composer, AWS Lambda, etc.) and for 3rd party tools (Fivetran, Hevo) which scale automatically as your data needs grow.
- Regularly monitor pipeline performance to identify and resolve scalability issues.
- Ensure tools are compatible with new data sources as they are added.

Example: A fast-growing media startup uses Google Cloud Composer to collect data from multiple social media platforms and scale data ingestion as their audience base expands.

6. Track Metadata and Maintain an Audit Trail

Metadata provides context about your data (e.g., when it was collected, where it came from, who accessed it). An audit trail helps troubleshoot issues and ensures compliance with regulations.

How to Do It:

- Implement metadata tracking and maintain logs of data collection events, including timestamps, data source IDs, and user actions.
- Periodically review logs to identify inconsistencies or unauthorized access.

Example: A logistics company uses metadata to track the origin of shipment data, ensuring accuracy when troubleshooting discrepancies.

7. Monitor Data Usage and Feedback

Regularly reviewing how the collected data is used ensures alignment with business needs. It also allows you to adjust collection processes to fill gaps or remove redundant data.

How to Do It:

- Conduct quarterly reviews with stakeholders to evaluate the relevance of the collected data.
- Use monitoring tools to track data pipeline performance and usage patterns.
- Solicit feedback from end-users (e.g., analysts or department heads) to identify missing or redundant data.

Example: A fintech startup notices analysts frequently request transaction metadata that isn't currently collected. They adjust their collection tools to include this data moving forward.

8. Optimize for Cost-Efficiency

Inefficient data collection processes can incur unnecessary storage and processing costs. Streamlining collection ensures you maximize ROI.

How to Do It:

- Use tiered storage solutions for collected data (e.g., move less-used data to cheaper storage options).
- Regularly audit your collection tools and processes for cost savings.
- De-duplicate data and remove irrelevant fields during the collection stage.

Example: A marketing startup identifies rarely used data fields in their collection process and eliminates them, saving on storage costs.

2.2.3 Data Processing

Data processing is the critical step of transforming raw, unorganized data into a structured, usable format for storage and analysis. It ensures the quality, accuracy, and consistency of the data before it flows downstream in the pipeline.

I recommend using ELT(Extract, Load, Transform) approach instead of usual ETL(Extract, Transform, Load) approach. In the ELT (Extract, Load, Transform) model, data processing at the pipeline stage focuses on extracting raw data from various sources and loading it into a storage system with minimal transformation. The goal is to preserve the raw format of the data as strings or general types, deferring complex transformations to the warehousing stage. This approach simplifies data ingestion, improves flexibility, and allows for robust transformation workflows later.

Why ELT Over ETL?

- **Flexibility**: Raw data is preserved, enabling future reprocessing if requirements change.
- **Scalability**: Simplifies pipelines by reducing processing at the ingestion stage, making it easier to scale.
- **Centralized Transformations**: Warehousing tools like BigQuery, dbt, and Snowflake are better suited for complex transformations and aggregations.

Recommendation: Load raw data into the warehouse as strings or basic types (e.g., integers, dates) without extensive cleaning or transformation during ingestion.

Key Activities in Data Processing (ELT)

1. *Data Cleaning (Minimal)*

   - Perform only basic cleaning tasks to ensure the raw data is usable enough for storage.
   - Basic cleaning ensures the data can be loaded into storage without breaking pipelines.
   - **Tasks Involved**:
     - Removing duplicate records at the source level, if possible.
     - Ensuring required fields (e.g., primary keys) are not null.
     - Standardizing encoding (e.g., UTF-8) for consistency.

   Example:
   An e-commerce platform checks that all transaction IDs are unique and standardizes date fields to avoid parsing errors during ingestion.

2. *Data Loading*

   - Import data into a data warehouse or storage system without altering its structure or format.
   - By importing raw data as-is, you retain the flexibility to define transformations later based on business needs.
   - **Tasks Involved**:
     - Load all fields as strings or general types (e.g., `VARCHAR` in SQL) to preserve raw data.
     - Avoid modifying or aggregating data during the loading phase.

   Example:
   A subscription service loads customer names, payment details, and timestamps directly into Snowflake, with no formatting changes.

Why ELT Works Better for Startups

1. **Preserves Original Data**: Storing raw data ensures you can re-process or re-analyze it if business questions evolve.

2. **Reduces Complexity**: Eliminates the need for heavy processing logic in the pipeline, simplifying maintenance.

3. **Leverages Advanced Warehousing Tools**: Warehousing platforms like BigQuery**,** Snowflake, and Redshift provide robust tools for cleaning, transforming, and analyzing data.

Tools for ELT-Based Data Processing

1. **Orchestration Tools**:
    - **Apache Airflow**: Schedule and automate data ingestion workflows.
    - **Prefect**: A modern tool for orchestrating lightweight ELT pipelines.

2. **Data Extraction Tools**:
    - **In-house Python Scripts or 3rd parties like Fivetran/Stitch Data**: Automate data extraction from various sources and load it into your warehouse.

3. **Python Libraries (for Custom Scripts)**:
    - **Pandas**: Handle basic cleaning before loading data into storage.
    - **PySpark**: For large-scale ingestion tasks.

Best Practices for Data Processing with ELT

1. **Focus on Raw Data at Ingestion**
   - Load all fields as strings or basic types (e.g., `VARCHAR`) to retain flexibility for later transformations.
   - Include metadata (e.g., source system, ingestion timestamp) to track the origin of each record.

2. **Validate Data Minimalistically**
   - Ensure no critical fields (e.g., primary keys) are missing.
   - Use lightweight validation rules to catch errors without blocking ingestion.

3. **Defer Complex Transformations**
   - Leave tasks like aggregation, categorization, and derived metrics for the warehousing stage.
   - Use warehousing tools like BigQuery for SQL-based transformations.

4. **Automate and Monitor the Pipeline**
   - Use orchestration tools like Airflow or Prefect to schedule data ingestion jobs.
   - Monitor ingestion pipelines to quickly detect and fix failures.

Example: A SaaS Startup Use Case

Scenario:
A SaaS company collects subscription and user activity data from multiple sources.

Steps in ELT Processing:

1. **Extract and Load**:
    - Subscription data (e.g., customer names, payment history) is loaded into BigQuery as-is, with all fields stored as strings.
    - User activity data is ingested from Firebase into BigQuery, retaining raw JSON format.

2. **Transformation (Deferred)**:
    - Later, in the warehousing stage, fields like `timestamp` are converted to ISO date formats, and payment data is enriched with currency conversions.

Outcome:
The company minimizes pipeline complexity and retains flexibility for future transformations and analytics.

Key Takeaway

Adopting an ELT approach allows startups to simplify data pipelines by focusing on extracting and loading raw data. Transformations are deferred to the warehousing stage, where tools like **databricks**, **BigQuery**, or **Snowflake** provide the flexibility to customize data for evolving business needs. This strategy reduces upfront effort, improves scalability, and ensures raw data is always available for reprocessing.

2.2.4 Data Storage

Data storage is the process of storing collected and minimally processed data in a centralized, scalable, and secure system. A well-designed storage solution ensures that data is easily accessible for analysis, reporting, and future use.

Types of Storage Systems

1. **Data Warehouses**
   - **Purpose**: Designed for structured, high-performance analytics use cases.
   - **Characteristics**: Optimized for query performance and scalability; ideal for structured datasets.
   - **Examples**:
     - **Google BigQuery**: A serverless, scalable warehouse that integrates seamlessly with Google Cloud products and supports ELT workflows.
     - **Snowflake**: Known for its scalability and ease of use, with strong support for multi-cloud environments.
     - **Amazon Redshift**: A cloud data warehouse suitable for medium to large-scale analytics projects.
   - **Use Case**: An e-commerce startup uses BigQuery to analyze website traffic and sales trends across regions.

2. **Databases**
   - **Purpose**: Used for storing structured operational data that requires frequent updates (e.g., transactional or real-time data).
   - **Characteristics**: Suitable for managing day-to-day operations; optimized for CRUD (Create, Read, Update, Delete) operations.
   - **Examples**:
     - **PostgreSQL**: A versatile open-source relational database system for structured data.
     - **MongoDB**: A NoSQL database for flexible, schema-less storage, suitable for semi-structured data.
   - **Use Case**: A SaaS startup stores customer information, billing details, and subscription plans in PostgreSQL.

3. **Data Lakes**
   - **Purpose**: Designed for storing raw, unstructured, or semi-structured data at scale.
   - **Characteristics**: Allows businesses to store data in its native format until needed; typically used for big data and advanced analytics.
   - **Examples**:
     - **Google Cloud Storage (GCS)**: A highly scalable and secure object storage service.
     - **AWS S3**: An industry-standard for object storage, supporting integration with big data tools.
   - **Use Case**: A media company stores large video files and log data in GCS for future AI-driven content analysis.

Why It's Important

1. **Centralized Data Access**:
   - A single source of truth eliminates data silos, ensuring all teams can access consistent information.
2. **Scalability**:
   - Modern storage systems scale effortlessly to accommodate growing data volumes without performance degradation.
3. **Security and Compliance**:
   - Centralized storage solutions provide robust security features, including encryption, role-based access control, and compliance with regulations like GDPR.
4. **Improved Analytics**:
   - Organized and structured data enables faster queries, accurate reporting, and actionable insights.

Examples

1. **Scenario 1: A SaaS Startup**
   - **Challenge**: The startup collects user behavior data from its app but struggles to manage and analyze it effectively.
   - **Solution**:
     - Loads raw user behavior data into **Google Cloud Storage** (data lake).
     - Processes and organizes the data into **BigQuery** (data warehouse) for analytics, generating insights into feature usage and customer retention.

2. **Scenario 2: A Retail Business**
   - **Challenge**: The company needs to store daily transactions while maintaining high performance for operational systems.
   - **Solution**:
     - Uses **PostgreSQL** for transactional data like customer orders.
     - Exports key metrics to **Snowflake** for in-depth sales analysis and reporting.

Best Practices for Data Storage

1. **Choose the Right Storage Type**
   - Use data warehouses for structured analytics, databases for operational data, and data lakes for unstructured/semi-structured data.
2. **Optimize for Cost-Efficiency**
   - Use tiered storage solutions (e.g., archival storage for infrequently accessed data) to minimize costs.
3. **Implement Access Controls**
   - Enforce role-based permissions to secure sensitive data.
4. **Monitor and Maintain**
   - Regularly review storage usage, optimize queries, and monitor for potential bottlenecks.
5. **Plan for Scalability**
   - Use cloud-native storage solutions like BigQuery, Snowflake, or AWS S3 to ensure seamless growth with your business.

Key Takeaway:

Data storage is the foundation of a scalable and efficient data strategy. Choosing the right storage system and following best practices ensures secure, organized, and accessible data, enabling meaningful analysis and driving business growth.

2.2.5 Data Orchestration

Data orchestration refers to the automated coordination, scheduling, and monitoring of data flows between different stages of a data pipeline, such as data collection, storage, processing, and loading into a data warehouse. Instead of manually handling these processes, orchestration ensures tasks are executed in the right order, at the right time, and with minimal human intervention.

At its core, data orchestration provides a framework to streamline workflows, manage dependencies between tasks, and ensure seamless operation of data pipelines in production.

Why Data Orchestration Matters

1. **Automation and Efficiency**
   - Orchestration eliminates the need for manual intervention by automating repetitive tasks like data ingestion, transformation, and storage.
   - Ensures that tasks are triggered automatically when certain conditions are met, such as data availability or time-based schedules.

2. **Error Handling and Monitoring**
   - Real-time alerts and monitoring help detect issues like pipeline failures, data inconsistencies, or delays.
   - Enables retries, rollbacks, or notifications if tasks fail to execute properly.

3. **Task Dependencies**
   - Manages dependencies between tasks to ensure data flows in the correct order. For instance, data cleaning must occur before transformation or storage.

4. **Scalability**
   - Orchestration frameworks can scale as your data grows, managing thousands of interconnected tasks across multiple systems.
5. **Reproducibility and Reliability**
   - Provides a single platform to monitor and control workflows, offering transparency and traceability.
6. **Error Reduction**
   - By removing human intervention, automation reduces errors such as duplicate records, inconsistent formats, or missed updates.
7. **Real-Time Insights**:
   - Data pipelines continuously process data, enabling organizations to make decisions based on up-to-date information.

Popular Data Orchestration Tools

1. **Apache Airflow**
   - **Overview**: Open-source workflow orchestration tool that uses Directed Acyclic Graphs (DAGs) to define workflows.
   - **Best For**: Complex, highly customized pipelines with dependencies across multiple systems.
   - **Hosting Options**:
     - Self-hosted on any infrastructure.
     - **Google Cloud Composer**: Fully managed Airflow environment on Google Cloud, ideal for users already in the Google ecosystem.
   - **Example Use Case**: A retail startup uses Airflow to schedule daily imports from CRM, clean the data, load it into BigQuery.

2. **Google Cloud Scheduler**
   - **Overview**: A lightweight, serverless option for scheduling batch jobs and triggering workflows in Google Cloud.
   - **Best For**: Simple pipelines or teams fully invested in the Google Cloud ecosystem.
   - **Example Use Case**: A small startup uses Cloud Scheduler to trigger a data ingestion script that updates a BigQuery dataset daily.

3. **Prefect**
   - **Overview**: A modern orchestration tool offering flexible workflows and cloud-native monitoring.
   - **Best For**: Teams looking for ease of use and a quick setup without sacrificing functionality.
   - **Key Feature**: Prefect's "flows" simplify pipeline design, and its cloud dashboard offers real-time visibility.
   - **Example Use Case**: A SaaS company uses Prefect to orchestrate nightly jobs that fetch subscription data, validate entries, and push updates to their dashboard.

4. **Dagster**
   - **Overview**: Focuses on data-aware orchestration, enabling fine-grained control over data transformations and metadata tracking.
   - **Best For**: Pipelines that require high observability and frequent iterations.
   - **Example Use Case**: A financial services startup uses Dagster to coordinate workflows across its data lake and warehouse, tracking changes at each stage.

Balanced Tool Selection

Recommendation: While **Apache Airflow on Google Cloud Composer** is an excellent choice for complex pipelines with tight Google Cloud integrations, the choice of orchestration tool depends on your startup's requirements:

- For a **Google Cloud-first approach**, prioritize **Cloud Composer** or **Google Cloud Scheduler**.
- For a quick-to-implement solution, consider **Prefect**.
- For high observability and advanced metadata tracking, **Dagster** may be ideal.

Key Takeaway for Data orchestration

Data orchestration is the backbone of a reliable pipeline. While **Apache Airflow on Google Cloud Composer** is a powerful and scalable option, tools like Prefect, Dagster, and Google Cloud Scheduler may be more suitable depending on your specific needs. By leveraging these tools effectively, startups can ensure smooth, automated, and scalable workflows.

Key Takeaway for considerations for data pipeline

A data pipeline is the **backbone of a data-driven startup**. It ensures your data is centralized, clean, and actionable—enabling **faster decisions**, greater efficiency, and scalability as your business grows.

The **core components of a data pipeline** are about efficiently moving data from its source to a centralized storage system while ensuring it is clean and organized. Startups can achieve this by combining automation tools, custom code, and scalable cloud infrastructure. These steps lay the groundwork for downstream activities like analytics and reporting, covered in later chapters.

1. **Data Collection**:
   - This stage involves gathering raw data from various sources, such as websites, mobile apps, IoT devices, databases, or APIs.
2. **Data Processing**:
   - Raw data is often messy and requires cleaning to remove duplicates, fix errors, and standardize formats.
   - Data is then transformed into a structured format
3. **Data Storage**:
   - The processed data is stored in a secure and accessible location, such as a data warehouse, database, or cloud storage.
   - This ensures scalability and provides a central repository for analysis.
4. **Data Orchestration**:
   - Automates the pipeline workflow, ensuring all tasks run smoothly and efficiently using tools like Apache Airflow or Google Cloud Composer.

By integrating these components, startups can automate, scale, and maintain their data operations effectively, ensuring reliable insights for decision-making.

2.3 Steps to Design a Basic Pipeline

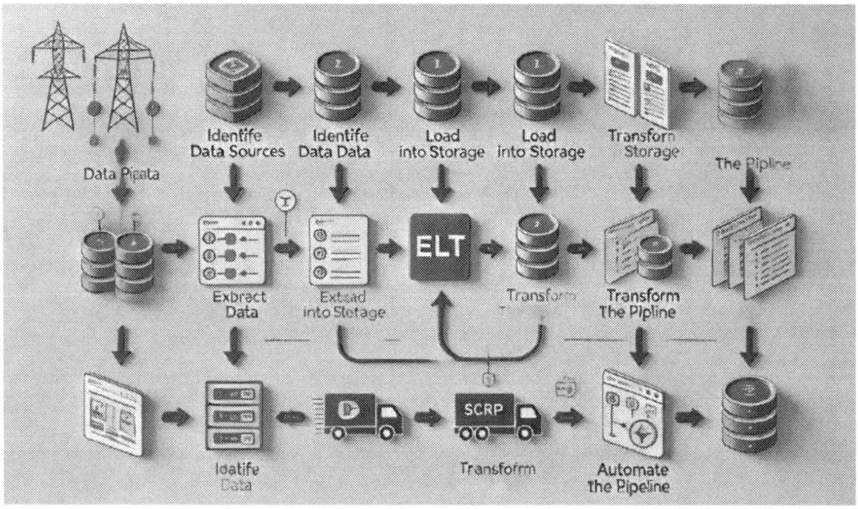

Building a data pipeline requires a structured approach to ensure it is scalable, efficient, and aligned with your business goals. Below are the high-level steps to design a pipeline using the ELT approach:

Step 1: Identify Your Data Sources

- List all sources of data your business generates or interacts with, such as:
  - **Web and App Analytics**: Google Analytics, Firebase.
  - **Operational Data**: Databases, APIs (e.g., Shopify, Stripe).
  - **External Platforms**: Google Play Console, Apple App Store.
- Ensure these sources support integration via APIs, exports, or data connectors.

Tip: Prioritize automating data extraction to minimize manual effort.

Step 2: Extract Data

- Use tools or scripts to extract raw data from your identified sources.
  - **No-Code Tools**: Fivetran, Stitch (for rapid integration).
  - **Code-Based Solutions**: Python libraries like `requests` or `pandas` for custom extractions.
- Schedule extractions to run regularly using orchestration tools like **Google Cloud Scheduler** or **Airflow**.

Best Practice: Log extraction times and metadata (e.g., record counts) to ensure consistency and traceability.

Step 3: Load Data into a Centralized Storage System

- Choose a scalable storage solution for raw data:
  - **Data Warehouses**: Google BigQuery, Snowflake (for structured analytics).
  - **Data Lakes**: Google Cloud Storage, AWS S3 (for unstructured or semi-structured data).
- Load data as-is (e.g., in string format) to preserve flexibility for future transformations.
- Loading raw data first allows you to handle transformations later, giving you more flexibility as your needs evolve.

Step 4: Transform Data

- Perform transformations directly within the data warehouse or storage system to simplify workflows.
  - Use **dbt (Data Build Tool)** for SQL-based transformations.
  - Rely on warehouse-native capabilities like BigQuery SQL for quick aggregations or enrichments.
- Typical transformations include:
  - Standardizing field names or formats.
  - Adding derived metrics (e.g., calculating retention rates).
  - Filtering out invalid or duplicate records.

Key Tip: Document transformation logic for future audits and reproducibility.

Step 5: Automate the Pipeline

- Orchestrate the entire workflow using tools like:
  - **Apache Airflow on Google Cloud Composer**: For complex workflows with dependencies.
  - **Prefect**: For quick-to-implement, user-friendly orchestration.
- Set up monitoring and alerts to track pipeline health and performance.

Why These Steps Are Necessary

1. **Delivers Consistent Data**: Automates repetitive tasks, reducing the risk of errors.
2. **Scales with Your Business**: Can accommodate growing data volumes and sources.
3. **Supports Flexible Analysis**: Leaves raw data intact for reprocessing or new transformations.

2.4 Summary of Tools and Platforms

This tabular format organizes tools by their categories (Storage, Orchestration, Transformation, etc.), making it easier to identify their purpose, suitability, and examples of how they can be used.

2.4.1 Data Storage and Warehousing

Tools/ Platform	**Overview**	**Best For**	**Example Use Case**
Google BigQuery	A serverless, fully-managed data warehouse optimized for analytics.	Cost-efficient and scalable analytics for large datasets.	An e-commerce startup stores user behavior data in BigQuery to analyze shopping trends.
Amazon Redshift	A cloud-native data warehouse integrated with AWS services.	AWS ecosystem users needing strong integration and reporting.	A SaaS company uses Redshift to analyze customer engagement alongside operational data.
Snowflake	A multi-cloud data warehouse with separate storage and compute layers for flexibility and cost efficiency.	Teams requiring multi-cloud compatibility and cross-team collaboration	A media company processes video analytics and shares data insights with global partners using Snowflake.

2.4.2 Data Orchestration

Tools/ Platform	Overview	Best For	Example Use Case
Apache Airflow (Cloud Composer)	An open-source workflow orchestration tool hosted on Google Cloud Composer for seamless cloud integration.	Complex workflows requiring Google Cloud integration.	A startup automates daily data ingestion and cleaning with Airflow, triggering SQL queries in BigQuery.
Prefect	A lightweight, modern orchestration tool with a cloud-native dashboard for monitoring.	Simple workflows and teams needing a quick-to-implement solution.	A fintech company schedules nightly ETL workflows for transaction analysis using Prefect.
Dagster	A data-aware orchestration tool designed for tracking metadata and providing high observability.	Pipelines requiring detailed tracking and metadata management.	A healthcare startup manages complex workflows across databases and analytical models with Dagster.
Google Cloud Scheduler	A serverless scheduling tool for triggering workflows and batch jobs.	Lightweight, time-based triggers within Google Cloud.	A small startup triggers ingestion tasks daily, uploading customer interaction data to BigQuery using Cloud Scheduler.

2.4.3 Data Transformation

Tools/ Platform	Overview	Best For	Example Use Case
dbt (Data Build Tool)	A SQL-based transformation framework designed for managing transformations in data warehouses.	Teams building repeatable and auditable transformation workflows.	A marketing team enriches campaign data with customer segmentation fields using dbt in BigQuery.
Python Libraries (e.g., Pandas)	Python-based libraries for small-scale transformations and preprocessing.	Smaller datasets or custom preprocessing tasks.	A data analyst preprocesses inventory data using Pandas before storing it in Snowflake.
PySpark	A distributed data processing engine for transforming large-scale datasets.	Large-scale, distributed transformations for big data.	A retail company uses PySpark to process transactional logs before loading them into BigQuery.

2.4.4 Data Integration

Tools/ Platform	Overview	Best For	Example Use Case
Fivetran	A fully-managed data integration platform with pre-built connectors for popular APIs and platforms.	Plug-and-play data ingestion from multiple sources.	A retail business pulls data from Shopify and Zendesk into BigQuery using Fivetran.
Stitch	A lightweight data pipeline tool designed for syncing data from sources to warehouses.	Budget-conscious teams needing simple data integration.	A startup syncs CRM data from HubSpot to Snowflake using Stitch.

2.4.5 Streaming and Batch Processing

Tools/ Platform	Overview	Best For	Example Use Case
Google Cloud Dataflow	A fully-managed service for real-time streaming and batch data processing.	Teams needing low-latency workflows for streaming data.	A logistics company processes real-time IoT data from delivery vehicles using Dataflow.
Amazon Athena	A serverless query engine for ad-hoc analysis of data stored in S3.	Ad-hoc querying of raw data in AWS environments.	An ad-tech startup queries raw ad impression logs stored in S3 using Athena to explore performance patterns.

2.5 Avoiding Common Pipeline Pitfalls

Building and maintaining data pipelines can be challenging, and even small issues can disrupt workflows or compromise data quality. Below are key pitfalls to watch for and strategies to address them effectively:

1. Data Loss During Transformation

- **Issue:** Errors during cleaning or transformation (e.g., incorrect mappings, data type mismatches) can result in missing or corrupted data.
- **Solution:**
  - **Validation Layers**: Implement pre- and post-transformation validation layers to ensure data consistency.
  - **Recommended Tools**: Use frameworks like **Great Expectations** to automate data validation checks.
  - **Best Practice**: Log transformation steps for traceability and create backups before modifying raw data.

Example:
A retail startup ensures data validation by using Great Expectations to detect null values in sales records after transformation.

2. Scalability Issues

- **Issue:** Pipelines designed for small datasets may fail or experience bottlenecks as data volumes increase.
- **Solution:**
    - Adopt **cloud-native solutions** like **Google BigQuery** or **Snowflake** that auto-scale to handle larger datasets.
    - Design modular pipelines where components can scale independently.
    - Use partitioning and clustering in data warehouses to improve query efficiency.

Example:
A media company migrates from on-premise ETL workflows to BigQuery for scalable processing of streaming data from multiple regions.

3. Complex and Disconnected Systems

- **Issue:** Using multiple tools without proper integration can lead to inefficiencies, increased latency, and troubleshooting challenges.
- **Solution:**
    - **Standardize Ecosystem**: Consolidate tools within a single cloud platform (e.g., Google Cloud or AWS).
    - **Integration-Friendly Tools**: Use orchestration tools like **Apache Airflow** to connect disparate systems seamlessly.
    - **Documentation**: Maintain clear documentation of all pipeline components and their interactions.

Example:
An IoT startup integrates all workflows into Google Cloud, using Cloud Storage, Pub/Sub, and BigQuery for end-to-end processing.

Unavoidable Challenges

While many pitfalls can be mitigated, some challenges require ongoing vigilance:

1. Latency and Slow Pipelines

- **Issue:** Delays in pipeline execution reduce the value of real-time insights, frustrating decision-makers.
- **Solution:**
  - Optimize ETL or ELT workflows by avoiding unnecessary transformations during data ingestion.
  - Use parallel processing frameworks like **Apache Beam** or **Google Cloud Dataflow** for faster computation.
  - Schedule jobs efficiently using tools like **Apache Airflow** or **Google Cloud Scheduler** to avoid bottlenecks.

Example:
A logistics company achieves near real-time reporting by running data ingestion and transformation tasks in parallel using Cloud Dataflow.

2. Backend Changes Affecting Pipelines

- **Issue:** Backend raw tables may be edited, modified, or appended with new columns, causing pipeline failures or incorrect outputs.
- **Solution:**
  - Regularly monitor and document schema changes.
  - Use schema-agnostic ingestion tools like **Fivetran** or **Stitch** to handle evolving table structures.
  - Implement automated alerts for schema changes.

Example:
A subscription-based app uses Fivetran to handle schema changes when new columns are added to its customer database.

3. Untriggered Jobs Due to Cloud Issues

- **Issue:** Pipeline jobs may fail to trigger due to server issues or misconfigurations in the cloud.
- **Solution:**
  - Set up monitoring tools like **Google Cloud Monitoring** or **Datadog** to detect and alert for pipeline failures.
  - Implement retry mechanisms in orchestration workflows to handle transient cloud issues.
  - Maintain redundancy by hosting critical components across multiple zones or regions.

Example:
A fintech startup mitigates downtime by using Airflow's retry policies to re-trigger failed ingestion tasks.

Best Practices to Mitigate Pitfalls

1. **Validate Early and Often**: Incorporate validation checks at every stage, from ingestion to storage.
2. **Build for Scale**: Design pipelines to handle future growth, using scalable tools like BigQuery and Snowflake.
3. **Monitor and Alert**: Use robust monitoring tools to catch and resolve pipeline failures quickly.
4. **Automate Workflows**: Automate scheduling and retries with orchestration tools like Airflow or Prefect.
5. **Keep It Simple**: Avoid unnecessary complexity by using unified ecosystems and modular pipeline designs.

Key Takeaway
By anticipating and addressing common pipeline pitfalls, startups can build robust, efficient, and scalable pipelines that minimize disruptions and maximize data value. A proactive approach to monitoring, validation, and automation ensures pipelines remain reliable even as data needs grow.

2.6 Conclusion: Building Data Pipelines

We discussed the pivotal role of data pipelines in a startup's journey to becoming data-driven. We explored how pipelines streamline the flow of data from diverse sources into centralized storage, ensuring it is consistent, scalable, and ready for analysis. The ELT (Extract, Load, Transform) approach emerged as a preferred methodology for startups, offering flexibility by loading raw data into warehouses before performing transformations. This allows startups to adapt to changing requirements and maintain data integrity.

By breaking down the essential steps to design a pipeline, we established a practical guide—from identifying data sources to implementing automated workflows with orchestration tools. Additionally, we addressed common pitfalls such as scalability challenges, data loss, and latency, equipping readers with strategies to build robust and efficient pipelines.

With a solid understanding of pipelines, you are now ready to take the next step: centralizing your data in a well-designed warehouse. Next Chapter will delve into the role of data warehousing in startups, helping you create a scalable and organized system that transforms raw data into actionable insights.

Chapter Three: Data Warehousing

Foundation of Scalable *Data Platforms*

Chapter Three: Data Warehousing

(Foundation Of Scalable Data Platforms)

A Data Warehouse is the cornerstone of a startup's data strategy, serving as the centralized hub where all structured data is stored, organized, and analyzed. It ensures scalability, streamlined access to insights, and cost efficiency. In modern data environments, a Data Warehouse also plays a critical role within a broader Data Platform, which integrates data lakes, real-time processing frameworks, and advanced analytics tools to support diverse data types and dynamic business needs. It ensures scalability, streamlined access to insights, and cost efficiency, while also playing a foundational role within broader Data Platforms, which integrate tools and technologies like data lakes, real-time processing frameworks, and AI-driven analytics. It ensures scalability, streamlined access to insights, and cost efficiency. In today's complex data environments, a Data Warehouse also plays a foundational role within broader Data Platforms, working alongside data lakes, real-time processing tools, and visualization systems to offer comprehensive insights.

Modern Data Warehouses, such as Snowflake and BigQuery, act as key components of Data Platforms, integrating seamlessly with data lakes for unstructured data, pipelines for real-time ingestion, and AI-driven tools for advanced insights. These capabilities ensure that organizations can scale efficiently while leveraging their data to drive impactful decisions.

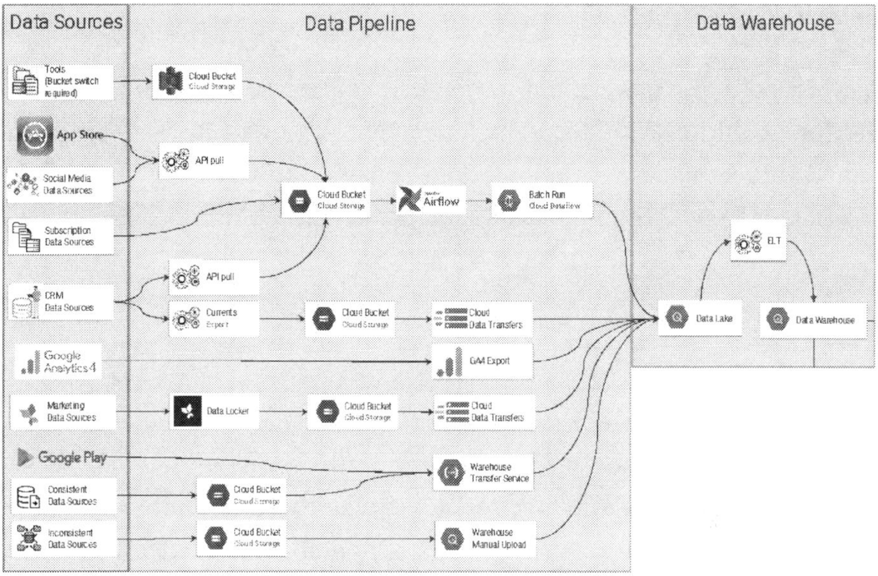

3.1 Introduction to Data Warehousing

A data warehouse is a centralized system designed to store, manage, and analyze large volumes of data. Unlike operational databases, which focus on real-time transactions, a data warehouse aggregates and organizes data for analytics and decision-making. It enables businesses to consolidate data from multiple sources into a single repository, transforming raw information into actionable insights.

3.2 Importance of Data Warehousing

Data warehousing is a critical component of modern business operations, offering solutions to data management challenges and enabling organizations to achieve their strategic goals. Below are the key reasons why data warehousing is essential, along with the problems it solves:

1. Centralization

One of the most significant benefits of a data warehouse is the ability to centralize data. By consolidating information from various sources—such as customer relationship management (CRM) tools, marketing platforms, web analytics, and operational databases—a data warehouse creates a unified and cohesive source of truth.

- **Problem Solved**: Disparate and siloed data systems make it challenging to gain a holistic view of operations.
- **How It Helps**: With centralized data, businesses can analyze their performance comprehensively, leading to more informed decision-making.

2. Scalability

As organizations grow, their data volumes and processing requirements increase exponentially. Data warehouses are designed to handle this growth seamlessly. Modern cloud-native solutions like Google BigQuery and Snowflake offer elastic scalability, enabling businesses to manage spikes in data and computational demands without costly infrastructure upgrades.

- **Problem Solved**: Traditional systems struggle to scale with growing data volumes, resulting in slow queries and increased maintenance costs.
- **How It Helps**: Scalable data warehouses ensure smooth performance and allow businesses to focus on growth without worrying about technological limitations.

3. Analytics-Ready Data

Data warehouses are specifically built for analytical workloads, making them ideal for querying, visualization, and reporting. By pre-aggregating, organizing, and structuring data into logical schemas, warehouses ensure that data is analytics-ready.

- **Problem Solved**: Raw data is often unstructured, inconsistent, or scattered across systems, making it difficult to analyze directly.
- **How It Helps**: With clean, structured, and organized data, businesses can quickly derive actionable insights, such as customer segmentation, trend forecasting, and performance tracking.

3.3 Key Features of Data Warehousing:

Data warehouses are designed with specific attributes that make them highly effective for analytics and decision-making. These features address the unique challenges of handling large volumes of data and delivering actionable insights efficiently:

1. Historical Data Storage

A defining feature of data warehouses is their ability to store vast amounts of historical data. Unlike operational databases that focus on current transactions, data warehouses retain past data, enabling businesses to analyze trends over time and make predictions. In a modern Data Platform, a data warehouse works alongside data lakes to complement its capabilities. While the data warehouse handles structured and analytics-ready data, the data lake stores unstructured and semi-structured data, such as logs or multimedia files, enabling a more comprehensive approach to data storage and analysis.

- **What It Enables**:
  - **Trend Analysis**: Understanding patterns such as seasonal sales fluctuations or long-term customer behavior.
  - **Predictive Modeling**: Using historical data to forecast future outcomes, such as demand for a product or churn rates.
- **Example**: A retail company might analyze five years of sales data in the data warehouse while combining it with customer sentiment data stored in the data lake to forecast inventory needs for the upcoming holiday season.

2. Fast Query Performance

Data warehouses are built to handle complex queries on large datasets with speed and efficiency. This is achieved through optimization techniques such as indexing, partitioning, and clustering. In a Data

Platform, real-time pipelines continuously feed data into the warehouse, ensuring that it remains up-to-date and ready for low-latency queries.

- **Key Techniques**:
  - **Indexing**: Organizing data for quicker retrieval.
  - **Partitioning**: Dividing data into logical segments, such as by date or region, to speed up specific queries.
  - **Clustering**: Grouping similar records together for efficient access.
- **What It Enables**: Near real-time querying, even when handling terabytes of data, , enabling operational dashboards and time-sensitive decision-making.
- **Example**: An e-commerce company can generate hourly sales trends for a flash sale campaign by querying real-time data ingested through streaming pipelines.

3. Separation from Operational Systems

By separating analytical workloads from transactional systems, data warehouses ensure that performance bottlenecks are avoided. Operational systems handle real-time transactions like order placement or payment processing, while analytical systems process large-scale queries for reporting and analysis.

- **Why It Matters**:
  - Prevents analytical queries from slowing down real-time transactions.
  - Allows uninterrupted reporting and dashboard updates, even during peak operational hours.
- **Example**: A subscription-based platform can analyze churn trends in its warehouse without impacting the real-time subscription billing system.

3.4 Selecting the Right Data Warehouse

Selecting the right data warehouse is a critical decision for any organization embarking on its data journey. A modern data warehouse should not only handle structured data but also integrate seamlessly into a broader Data Platform, enabling collaboration with data lakes, real-time processing tools, and visualization platforms. The right platform can streamline operations, optimize performance, and reduce costs. When evaluating data warehouse platforms, consider the following key factors:

1. **Scalability**: The ability to handle growing data volumes and query loads without performance degradation. Ensure the platform supports elastic scaling and integrates with real-time pipelines and data lakes for comprehensive data management.
2. **Ease of Use**: Intuitive interfaces, documentation, and support for SQL and other languages.
3. **Performance**: Query execution times, support for concurrent users, and real-time data processing capabilities. Evaluate the platform's ability to handle streaming data and its efficiency in feeding insights into dashboards and AI-driven workflows.
4. **Integration**: Seamless connectivity with other components of a Data Platform, such as data lakes for unstructured data, real-time ingestion pipelines, and AI/ML frameworks for advanced analytics. Look for native support for cloud services and multi-cloud compatibility.
5. **Cost**: Pricing models that align with your organization's budget and usage patterns. Consider cost-efficiency in both storage and compute, especially in a Data Platform that may include multiple tools like data lakes and processing frameworks.

Below is a detailed comparison of four leading data warehousing platforms: Google BigQuery, Databricks, Amazon Redshift, and Snowflake.

Detailed Comparison Table

Feature	**Google BigQuery**	**Databricks**	**Amazon Redshift**	**Snowflake**
Scalability	Serverless, auto-scales seamlessly for any workload.	Highly scalable, designed for large-scale data and ML workloads.	Requires manual resizing; auto-scaling available in Redshift Serverless.	Elastic scaling with no downtime.
Ease of Use	Intuitive for Google Cloud users; fully managed.	Requires knowledge of Spark for advanced use.	Tailored for AWS ecosystem users; moderate learning curve.	User-friendly interface, ideal for non-technical users.
Performance	Optimized for high-concurrency analytics.	Exceptional performance for ML and ETL tasks; supports streaming data.	High performance depends on cluster size and configuration.	Excellent concurrency and query speed for analytical workloads.
Integration	Native integration with Google Cloud products and BI tools like Looker.	Supports integrations with Spark, ML frameworks, and cloud services.	Strong integration with AWS services (S3, Glue, Athena).	Multi-cloud support; integrates with major BI tools.
Storage Format	Columnar storage optimized for analytics.	Supports structured, semi-structured, and unstructured data.	Columnar storage for fast query performance.	Optimized for structured and semi-structured data.

Feature	**Google BigQuery**	**Databricks**	**Amazon Redshift**	**Snowflake**
Machine Learning Support	Limited native ML capabilities but integrates with Vertex AI.	Strong ML support with built-in libraries and frameworks like TensorFlow.	Limited ML support; requires external tools.	Limited native ML; integrates with external tools.
Pricing	Pay-per-query model; cost-effective for smaller workloads.	Pay-as-you-go or reserved clusters for predictable costs.	Hourly billing for clusters; Redshift Serverless offers on-demand pricing.	Consumption-based pricing; compute and storage billed separately.
Compatibility (Cloud)	Google Cloud only.	Supports Azure, AWS, and GCP.	AWS only.	Fully multi-cloud (AWS, Azure, GCP).
Target Use Case	Best for analytics-focused workloads, real-time querying, and dashboarding.	Ideal for organizations with heavy ML, AI, or data engineering workloads.	Suitable for businesses already using AWS services.	Great for scalable analytics and collaboration across cloud platforms.
Unique Strengths	Serverless, low cost for querying large datasets.	Combines data engineering, analytics, and machine learning in one platform.	Tight integration with AWS for seamless workflows.	Automatic performance tuning and high concurrency.

3.5 Steps to Build a Data Warehouse

Building a data warehouse requires a structured approach to ensure that it meets the organization's needs for scalability, performance, and usability. Below are the detailed steps for creating a robust data warehouse:

1. Define Objectives

Start by identifying the purpose of the data warehouse and the specific business questions it will answer.

- **Example Objectives**:
  - Monitor sales performance across regions.
  - Track customer behavior and churn trends.
  - Generate reports on product profitability.
- **Outcome**: A clear understanding of the metrics, KPIs, and insights.

2. Design the Data Architecture

Organize your data warehouse using schemas that align with your business's specific needs and reflect your operational workflows. The proposed structure includes schemas for **Subscribers**, **Engagement**, **Catalogue**, and **Stores**, each designed to house relevant and logically grouped data.

a) Subscribers

This schema focuses on user account management, orders, and payment data. It provides insights into the lifecycle of a subscriber.

- **Core Tables**:
  - **Accounts**: Stores details about user profiles, registration dates, subscription tiers, and statuses (e.g., active, canceled).
  - **Orders**: Contains records of subscription purchases, renewals, and upgrades, including timestamps and order IDs.

  - **Payments**: Captures payment details such as transaction IDs, amounts, methods (e.g., card, PayPal), and payment statuses (e.g., success, failure).
- **Example Use Case**: Analyze the lifetime value (LTV) of subscribers by joining payment data with account details.

b) Engagement

Tracks user behavior across platforms, focusing on interactions and activity within your services.

- **Core Tables**:
  - **Session Logs**: Stores data about user sessions, such as session duration, timestamps, and device types.
  - **Feature Interactions**: Tracks engagement with specific app features or content, including click rates, video views, and likes.
  - **Retention Metrics**: Includes daily/weekly/monthly active users (DAU/WAU/MAU) and churn trends.
- **Example Use Case**: Identify features that drive the highest engagement or pinpoint churn-prone segments.

c) Catalogue

Holds data related to the products, services, or content offered by the business.

- **Core Tables**:
  - **Items**: Stores detailed information about offerings, such as product names, descriptions, pricing, and categories.
  - **Inventory**: Tracks availability, restocking schedules, and stock levels (if applicable).
  - **Ratings and Reviews**: Stores customer feedback and ratings to analyze product performance.
- **Example Use Case**: Perform an analysis to identify top-performing products or content based on sales or engagement data.

d) Stores (Apple/Google Store)

Centralizes data from app stores where your product is hosted, focusing on app-specific performance and monetization.

- **Core Tables**:
  - **Store Metrics**: Tracks downloads, updates, and uninstalls from platforms like Apple Store and Google Play.
  - **Revenue Reports**: Stores data about revenue generated from in-app purchases or subscriptions processed through the stores.
  - **Feedback and Reviews**: Contains user reviews, star ratings, and comments from app stores.
- **Example Use Case**: Identify trends in app performance and correlate store reviews with engagement or retention metrics.

Benefits of This Structure

This structure is designed to align with your data sources, ensuring that minimal transformation is needed when pulling data into the warehouse. It emphasizes efficiency, clarity, and the ability to derive actionable insights from the data.

- **Alignment with Data Sources**: Since the structure mirrors the original data sources (e.g., app stores, engagement metrics, catalog data), the data integration process is streamlined, reducing the need for complex transformations during the ELT process.
- **Clarity and Organization**: Dividing data into schemas such as **Subscribers**, **Engagement**, **Catalogue**, and **Stores** provides a logical separation, making the warehouse easier to navigate and reducing overall complexity.
- **Scalability**: The structure is flexible and can grow with your business. For example, you can easily add new tables (e.g., a new subscription tier) or expand existing ones (e.g., additional app stores or product categories).

- **Performance Optimization**: By organizing data around functional areas, queries can be optimized for specific use cases, such as analyzing engagement trends or catalog performance, ensuring faster response times.
- **Actionable Insights**: The structure supports cross-referencing between schemas for deeper analysis. For example:
  - Connect app store revenue data to engagement trends to identify high-performing platforms.
  - Analyze catalog performance alongside subscriber retention metrics to determine which products drive long-term engagement.

This approach ensures your data warehouse is both user-friendly and future-proof, enabling faster insights without unnecessary complexity.

3. Transform Data for Analytics

Transforming raw data into an analytics-ready format is a critical step in creating a high-performing data warehouse. This process ensures that data is standardized, meaningful, and accessible for teams across the organization.

Steps for Data Transformation

- **Standardization**
  - Convert all dates, currencies, and formats into consistent standards across datasets.
  - *Example*: Ensure all timestamps are in UTC, and monetary values are unified in the same currency.
- **Consolidation of Daily Data**
  - For datasets updated daily (e.g., transactional or engagement data), create consolidated tables that aggregate and organize data for historical analysis and ease of access.

  - Consolidation ensures that all teams have a single, reliable source of truth to work with.
- **Aggregation**
  - Summarize raw data into higher-level metrics to enable faster and more efficient analysis.
  - This often involves combining data from various sources, such as subscriber data, engagement data, catalog data, revenue data, and customer experience data.
  - *Example*: Calculate key metrics such as monthly sales, daily active users, or customer lifetime value (CLV).
- **Derived Fields**
  - Add new calculated fields to provide deeper insights and enhance decision-making.
  - *Example*: Generate fields like profit margins, retention rates, or engagement scores using existing data.

4. Optimize Performance with Indexing, Partitioning, and Clustering

Indexing, Partitioning, and Clustering are essential to ensure your warehouse operates efficiently even as data volumes grow:

- **Faster Queries**: By minimizing the data scanned during queries, performance improves significantly.
- **Lower Costs**: Efficient querying reduces processing costs, especially in platforms with pay-per-query pricing models like BigQuery.
- **Scalability**: These optimizations help maintain performance as data scales, ensuring the warehouse remains responsive.

Indexing:
- **What It Is**: Indexing involves creating a data structure to speed up query execution by allowing faster lookups.
- **Use Case**: Improve search efficiency in large tables.
- **Example**: Index a `CustomerID` column in a `Sales` table to accelerate customer-specific queries.

Partitioning:

- **What It Is**: Partitioning splits a table into smaller, logical segments based on a key, such as date or region.
- **Use Case**: Reduces the amount of data scanned during queries.
- **Example**: Partition a `Sales` table by `Region` to allow regional analysis without scanning the entire table.
- **Supported Platforms**: BigQuery and Snowflake offer automatic partitioning capabilities.

Clustering:

- **What It Is**: Clustering organizes data within partitions based on specific columns to improve query efficiency.
- **Use Case**: Boosts performance for queries involving range filters or grouping.
- **Example**: Cluster a `Transactions` table by `TransactionDate` and `CustomerID` to optimize customer-specific time-series queries.

Pro Tip: Use a combination of partitioning and clustering for best results. For example, partition a table by `Date` and cluster it by `Region` for fast filtering and aggregation.

5. Set Up Data Governance

Implementing robust data governance practices is critical for ensuring that your data remains secure, consistent, and compliant with regulations. Data governance involves setting rules, processes, and standards to manage your organization's data effectively throughout its lifecycle. Here's how to establish governance practices:

a) Access Controls

- **What It Is**: Role-based permissions that restrict access to sensitive data based on the user's role and responsibilities.
- **Why It's Important**: Prevents unauthorized access and ensures that only the right people have access to specific datasets. This is

particularly critical for maintaining compliance with privacy laws like GDPR and CCPA.

- **Best Practices**:
  - Use identity and access management tools like Google Cloud IAM or AWS IAM to implement granular permissions.
  - Define roles such as **Data Viewer**, **Data Editor**, and **Data Admin**, assigning them based on team requirements.
  - Mask sensitive fields (e.g., personally identifiable information or financial data) for non-privileged users.

b) Validation Rules

- **What It Is**: Quality checks that identify and flag anomalies in your data, such as duplicates, null values, or inconsistent formats.
- **Why It's Important**: Ensures the integrity and reliability of data, reducing errors during analysis and decision-making.
- **Best Practices**:
  - Define validation rules during data ingestion to check for expected formats, ranges, or completeness. For instance:
    - Ensure email fields contain valid email addresses.
    - Validate numerical data, such as prices or quantities, against predefined thresholds.
  - Conduct periodic data audits to identify issues that might slip through real-time validations.

c) Audit Logs

- **What It Is**: A mechanism to track all data changes, including modifications, deletions, and access attempts.
- **Why It's Important**: Provides accountability and transparency by maintaining a record of who accessed or altered data and when. This is essential for troubleshooting issues and maintaining compliance.
- **Best Practices**:
  - Enable audit logging in your cloud platform (e.g., BigQuery Audit Logs or AWS CloudTrail).

  - Regularly review logs to detect unauthorized access attempts or unusual activity.
  - Retain logs for a sufficient duration to comply with regulatory requirements, such as HIPAA or PCI DSS.

Additional Governance Practices

- **Data Cataloging**:
  - Create a metadata repository to document what each dataset contains, its purpose, and its owner. Tools like Google Data Catalog or AWS Glue can help.
- **Version Control for Data Models**:
  - Use version control for schemas and transformations to ensure reproducibility and rollback options in case of errors.
- **Compliance Monitoring**:
  - Implement tools that automate compliance checks against legal and industry standards to ensure adherence to privacy laws.

6. Load Data Incrementally

Incremental loading is a powerful approach to improve efficiency and minimize processing time by updating only new or changed data rather than reloading entire datasets.

Instead of loading the entire dataset repeatedly, incremental loading focuses on adding or updating only the records that have changed. This reduces system strain, accelerates processing, and ensures real-time or near-real-time data availability.

How It Works

- **Identify Changes**: Use a timestamp, unique key, or checksum to identify records that are new or have been updated.
- **Load Updates**: Pull only the identified records into the target data warehouse.

- **Automate the Process**: Set up workflows to trigger incremental updates at regular intervals or based on events.

Benefits

- **Efficiency**: Reduces data transfer and processing time, especially for large datasets.
- **Cost Savings**: Minimizes cloud storage and compute expenses by processing only what's necessary.
- **Timeliness**: Ensures fresh data is always available for analytics.

Incremental loading is a must for businesses with growing datasets or real-time analytics needs, making it a cornerstone of an efficient ELT strategy.

7. Monitor and Optimize

Regularly monitoring and optimizing your data warehouse ensures it performs efficiently and remains cost-effective as your data grows.

Continuous Monitoring

- **Performance Tracking**:
  - Use built-in monitoring dashboards in platforms like BigQuery, Snowflake, or Redshift to track query performance, data load times, and resource utilization.
  - Set up alerts for anomalies like failed queries or unusual usage spikes.
- **Cost Analysis**:
  - Monitor billing dashboards to identify cost-heavy queries or excessive storage usage.
  - Tools like Google Cloud Monitoring or Snowflake's Resource Monitor can help pinpoint inefficiencies.

Optimization Tips

- **Rewrite Slow Queries**:
  - Analyze query execution plans to identify bottlenecks and rewrite inefficient joins or aggregations.
  - Use partitioning or clustering to improve query performance for large datasets.
- **Remove Unused Assets**:
  - Periodically clean up unused tables, indexes, and views to reduce clutter and optimize storage.
  - Archive historical data that is rarely accessed but still needs to be retained.

- **Automate Maintenance**:
  - Schedule automated tasks like **vacuuming** (to reclaim storage space) or **defragmentation** to maintain optimal performance in Redshift.
  - For BigQuery and Snowflake, enable automatic data clustering and pruning features.
- **Optimize Storage Costs**:
  - Move cold or infrequently accessed data to cheaper storage tiers (e.g., BigQuery's long-term storage or Snowflake's Time Travel feature).
  - Compress data using built-in tools to reduce storage requirements.

By actively monitoring and optimizing your data warehouse, you can ensure it remains scalable, cost-efficient, and ready to support your organization's analytics needs.

3.6 Best Practices for Maintaining a Data Warehouse

Maintaining a data warehouse effectively is essential to ensure it remains scalable, reliable, and cost-efficient. By following these best practices, you can enhance the performance and longevity of your data infrastructure:

1. Monitor Performance Regularly

- Continuously track query execution times, storage usage, and data load speeds using built-in monitoring tools like BigQuery Monitoring, Snowflake Resource Monitor, or Redshift Console.
- Identify and address bottlenecks in real time to avoid disruptions.

2. Implement Data Governance

- **Access Control**: Restrict data access based on user roles to protect sensitive information. Use tools like Google Cloud IAM or Snowflake Access Control.
- **Data Quality Rules**: Set up automated validations during data ingestion to ensure consistent and accurate data.
- **Audit Logs**: Enable logging to track all changes, providing transparency and compliance with regulations like GDPR and CCPA.

3. Optimize Queries and Workloads

- Rewrite queries to minimize complexity, avoid unnecessary joins, and leverage **partitioning** and **clustering** for better performance.
- Schedule large queries or ETL jobs during off-peak hours to reduce resource contention.
- Use materialized views or summary tables for frequently accessed data.

4. Manage Storage Efficiently

- Archive historical or infrequently accessed data to cheaper storage tiers, such as BigQuery Long-Term Storage or S3 Glacier for Redshift.
- Regularly clean up unused tables, indexes, and intermediate files to reduce storage costs.
- Compress data where possible to save space.

5. Automate Maintenance Tasks

- Use automation tools to perform routine tasks such as vacuuming, defragmentation, and schema updates. For example:
  - **Redshift**: Automate `VACUUM` and `ANALYZE` commands.
  - **Snowflake**: Enable automatic clustering.
  - **BigQuery**: Use scheduled queries to maintain summary or aggregate tables.

6. Ensure Scalability

- Design your warehouse to scale as your data volume grows by leveraging cloud-native solutions like BigQuery or Snowflake, which offer elastic scalability.
- Regularly review usage patterns to adjust compute resources and ensure optimal performance during peak loads.

7. Backup and Disaster Recovery

- Implement automated backup solutions to protect against data loss.
- Use features like Snowflake's Time Travel or BigQuery's Versioned Tables for quick data recovery.
- Periodically test recovery plans to ensure minimal downtime during failures.

8. Document and Standardize Processes

- Maintain a data catalog to document schemas, tables, and their purposes. Use tools like Google Data Catalog or AWS Glue.
- Standardize naming conventions and column formats to improve collaboration and reduce confusion across teams.

9. Regularly Review Costs

- Monitor your billing dashboards to identify unnecessary expenses.
- Consolidate rarely accessed datasets or optimize ETL processes to reduce unnecessary compute and storage costs.
- Move non-critical workloads to cheaper tiers or adjust compute capacities as needed.

10. Plan for Growth

- Periodically review your architecture to ensure it aligns with business goals.
- Anticipate future requirements by designing flexible schemas that can accommodate new data sources or business changes.

By adhering to these best practices, your data warehouse will remain an efficient and powerful tool for analytics, enabling your organization to derive maximum value from its data.

3.7 Conclusion: Building a Data Warehouse

Building a data warehouse is a pivotal step in enabling data-driven decision-making for any organization. A well-structured and optimized warehouse acts as a centralized repository, consolidating data from disparate sources into a single source of truth. This not only simplifies access but also ensures that the data is consistent, secure, and analytics-ready.

Throughout this chapter, we explored the importance of data warehousing, its key features, and the step-by-step process to build and maintain one. From selecting the right platform to designing schemas, transforming data, and implementing governance, each step plays a critical role in ensuring the warehouse can scale with your business and provide actionable insights.

A successful data warehouse should not only support current business needs but also be adaptable to future growth and changes. Its integration with broader Data Platforms ensures long-term scalability and relevance by complementing tools like data lakes for unstructured data and real-time analytics frameworks for dynamic insights. By incorporating best practices like incremental loading, query optimization, and automated maintenance, organizations can ensure their warehouse remains efficient and cost-effective.

Whether you're a startup looking to establish a data foundation or a growing company aiming to enhance analytics capabilities, investing in a robust data warehouse is essential. It is the backbone of a data strategy that drives informed decisions, operational efficiency, and sustainable growth.

What to Expect in the Next Chapter

With your data warehouse in place, the next chapter will explore how to transform raw data into actionable insights through **dashboards and reporting**. We'll delve into:

1. **Designing Dashboards**: Principles of creating intuitive and visually impactful dashboards tailored to business needs.
2. **Selecting Visualization Tools**: A comparison of tools like Tableau, Looker, and Power BI to help you make the right choice.
3. **Automating Reports**: How to set up automated reporting systems for real-time decision-making.
4. **Key Metrics and KPIs**: Identifying the critical metrics that matter most to your organization and how to visualize them effectively.

This chapter will guide you in turning data into a strategic asset, helping your team understand trends, identify opportunities, and make informed decisions faster. Let's take the next step in unlocking the power of your data!

Chapter Four: Building Dashboards and Reports

Chapter Four: Building Dashboards and Reports

In this chapter, we explore how to transform raw data into actionable insights using dashboards and reporting tools. Dashboards provide a visual representation of critical metrics, empowering organizations to monitor performance, identify trends, and make informed decisions in real time. Effective dashboards are more than just charts—they are a bridge between complex data and actionable insights.

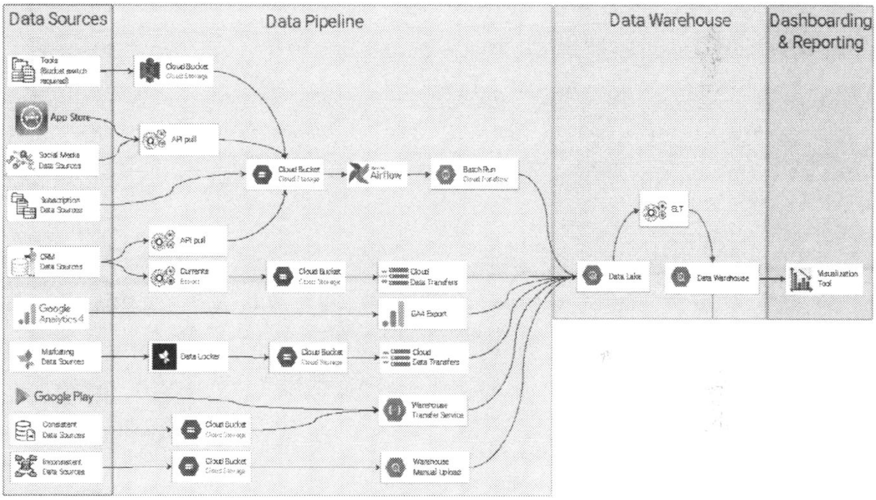

4.1 Importance of Dashboards

Dashboards are powerful tools that bridge the gap between raw data and actionable insights, providing organizations with the means to make informed decisions. They allow businesses to visualize complex datasets in an intuitive and centralized way, fostering a data-driven culture.

Here are the key benefits dashboards bring to organizations:

1. **Simplified Decision-Making**:
   - Dashboards aggregate data from various sources and present it in a visual format that is easy to interpret.
   - They help stakeholders quickly identify key trends, issues, and opportunities without delving into raw data.
2. **Real-Time Monitoring**:
   - With live data updates, dashboards enable organizations to track performance metrics as they happen.
   - This capability ensures timely responses to challenges and enhances operational agility.
3. **Improved Transparency and Collaboration**:
   - Dashboards act as a shared source of truth across teams, promoting alignment on goals and performance.
   - By democratizing access to data, they empower all departments to participate in data-driven discussions.
4. **Efficiency in Reporting**:
   - Automated dashboards eliminate the need for manual report generation, saving time and reducing errors.
   - They can be tailored to different audiences, from high-level summaries for executives to detailed views for analysts.
5. **Strategic Insights**:
   - Dashboards enable organizations to track KPIs, measure progress toward goals, and prioritize initiatives based on data.
   - They support strategic planning by uncovering patterns, forecasting trends, and benchmarking performance against industry standards.

In summary, dashboards are essential for turning data into actionable insights, fostering collaboration, and driving business success. By leveraging the right tools and design principles, organizations can maximize the impact of their data and stay competitive in a dynamic environment.

4.2 Principles of Effective Dashboard Design

Creating impactful dashboards requires careful planning and strategic alignment with organizational needs. A well-designed dashboard not only presents data visually but also facilitates actionable insights. Below are the key principles:

1. **Define Clear Objectives**:
   - Identify the purpose of the dashboard: Is it intended for operational monitoring, strategic decision-making, or project tracking?
   - Tailor the content to the audience. For instance, executives may prefer high-level KPIs, while analysts might require granular details.
   - Ensure that every visualization and metric aligns with the dashboard's goals, avoiding unnecessary clutter.

2. **Focus on Key Performance Indicators (KPIs)**:
   - Highlight KPIs that directly impact business objectives. For example, revenue growth, customer acquisition, or cost efficiency.
   - Limit the number of metrics displayed to avoid overwhelming users and emphasize clarity.
   - Categorize KPIs into thematic groups such as operational, financial, and customer-centric metrics for better navigation.

3. **Use Appropriate Visualizations**:
   - Choose visualization types based on the data and its context:
     - **Line Charts**: For trends over time (e.g., monthly sales).
     - **Bar Charts**: For category comparisons (e.g., regional performance).
     - **Heatmaps**: For intensity and anomaly detection (e.g., customer activity).
     - **Tables**: For detailed metrics requiring exact numbers.
   - Avoid visualizations like pie charts for datasets with numerous segments, as they can become difficult to interpret.
   - Use color strategically: green for positive trends, red for issues, and neutral tones for baseline data.

4. **Ensure Interactivity**:
   - Provide features like filters, drill-downs, and hover-to-explore options to allow users to customize their views.
   - Enable users to interact with data dynamically, such as filtering reports by date range, region, or product.
   - Allow exporting and saving customized reports for recurring use.

5. **Maintain Consistency**:
   - Apply a uniform color scheme, layout, and font style across all dashboards to build familiarity and enhance usability.
   - Group related metrics into sections to provide a logical flow. For instance, financial metrics should be placed together, followed by operational insights.
   - Use standardized terminologies and formats, such as consistent currency symbols and date structures.

6. **Structure Dashboards Logically**:
    - Organize dashboards by functional categories to meet the specific needs of various business areas. For example:
        - **Operational Metrics**: Track real-time metrics related to daily operations, such as server uptime, inventory levels, and delivery times. These dashboards enable operational teams to ensure smooth workflows and detect issues promptly.
        - **Customer Insights**: Focus on metrics for subscription, acquisition, and retention:
            1. **Subscription Metrics**: Include trial-to-subscription conversion rates, churn rates, and subscription revenue growth.
            2. **Acquisition Metrics**: Highlight customer acquisition costs (CAC), acquisition channels, and campaign effectiveness.
            3. **Retention Metrics**: Display customer lifetime value (CLV), repeat purchase rates, and retention by customer segment.
        - **Financial Performance**: Present revenue, expenses, profit margins, and cost analysis. These dashboards assist finance teams in tracking spending and ensuring profitability.
    - Use tabs or sections within dashboards to group functional areas logically, while maintaining a consistent and user-friendly flow.

7. **Real-Time and Scheduled Updates**:
    - Set up dashboards to refresh data based on the required cadence—real-time for operational metrics, hourly or daily for monitoring, and weekly or monthly for strategic reviews.
    - Clearly label the last updated time on the dashboard to build trust and ensure data relevance.

8. **Incorporate Alerts and Triggers**:
   - Add automated alerts to notify users of critical threshold breaches (e.g., revenue drop, increased churn).
   - Set triggers for anomalies, such as sudden changes in user activity, and integrate them with email or messaging systems.

9. **Include Cost Monitoring Dashboards**:
   - Design specific dashboards to track and manage costs across different business areas. For instance, display monthly cloud expenses or marketing campaign costs alongside performance metrics.
   - Use cost-monitoring dashboards to identify areas of overspending and suggest reallocation strategies.

10. **Enable Self-Serve Data Exploration**:
    - Empower users with self-serve tools to explore data independently. Provide features like drag-and-drop visualization builders, interactive filters, and pre-built templates for common use cases.
    - Offer training and documentation to make self-serve tools accessible for non-technical users.

By adhering to these principles, dashboards will not only convey insights effectively but also foster a culture of data-driven decision-making throughout the organization.

4.3 Selecting the Right Tools

Choosing the right dashboarding and reporting tool is a critical decision, as it directly impacts how efficiently data is analyzed and shared. The choice should balance the technical expertise, budget, and specific needs. Below are the key factors to consider and a detailed comparison of popular tools.

Factors to Consider:

1. **Technical Expertise**:
   - Evaluate whether your team has the necessary skills to handle advanced tools or requires something more user-friendly.
   - Advanced tools like Tableau and Looker may need some training.

2. **Integration Capabilities**:
   - Ensure the tool integrates seamlessly with your existing data sources, such as Google Analytics, CRM systems, or data warehouses like BigQuery.
   - My Recommendation: Tools like Looker excel in integrating with cloud platforms like Google Cloud, while Power BI integrates seamlessly with Microsoft products.

3. **Scalability**:
   - For startups expecting rapid growth, choose tools that can scale with increasing data complexity and user demands.
   - Tableau and Looker provide enterprise-grade scalability, while Google Data Studio is ideal for lighter workloads.

4. **Visualization Needs**:
   - Advanced analytics and interactivity might require a robust tool like Tableau or Power BI.
   - For basic reports and dashboards, Google Data Studio suffices and is cost-effective.

5. **Cost**:
   - Startups with limited budgets can begin with free or low-cost options like Google Data Studio.
   - As needs grow, transitioning to subscription-based tools with advanced features (e.g., Tableau, Looker) can provide additional value.

Comparison of Popular Tools

Choosing the right dashboarding and reporting tool is critical for startups as it directly affects how efficiently data is managed, analyzed, and shared. Below is the table for comparison of popular tools.

Tool	Best For	Key Features
Tableau	Advanced analytics	- Highly interactive and customizable dashboards. - Rich library of visualization types. - Robust scalability for large datasets. - Seamless integration with multiple data sources like SQL, spreadsheets, and APIs. - Cloud and on-premise options available. *- Cost: Subscription based*
Power BI	Microsoft ecosystem users	- Tight integration with Microsoft tools such as Excel, Azure, and Teams. - Built-in AI and machine learning capabilities. - Real-time analytics and automated insights. - Cost-effective for organizations already using Microsoft products. - Wide range of visual templates and customization options. *- Cost: Affordable with Free tier*
Looker	Google Cloud integration	- Advanced data modeling for structured and unstructured data. - Realtime and embedded analytics for applications. - Flexible API for integrating custom workflows. - Ideal for teams leveraging Google BigQuery and other Google Cloud tools. - Supports governed data exploration to ensure consistency across teams. *- Cost: Subscription based*
Google Data Studi	Beginners, light dashboards	- Free and beginner-friendly interface. - Easy integration with Google tools - Drag-and-drop report builder for simple dashboards. - Best for small-scale reporting and lightweight analysis. - No advanced customization or scalability compared to enterprise-grade tools. *- Cost: Free*

Practical Implementation Tips:

- **Start Simple**: Begin with tools that align with your current expertise and budget, such as Google Data Studio.
- **Invest in Training**: Allocate time for your team to learn the selected tool. Many platforms offer free resources or certifications (e.g., Tableau Public, Power BI tutorials).
- **Evaluate Periodically**: As your startup grows, reassess your needs and transition to more advanced tools if necessary.
- **Leverage Free Trials**: Many subscription-based tools offer free trials, which can help determine if the tool meets your specific requirements.

By carefully considering your startup's current and future needs, you can choose the right dashboarding tool to unlock the power of your data and enable better decision-making.

4.4 Building a Dashboard: Step-by-Step

A well-designed self-serve tool improves operational efficiency and empowers employees at all levels to make informed decisions based on data. Here is the step-by-step approach for building dashboards:

1. **Identify Key Metrics**:
    - Focus on metrics that directly impact business goals. Prioritize quality over quantity to avoid overwhelming users with unnecessary data.
    - For an e-commerce startup:
        - Conversion Rates: Track how effectively your website or platform turns visitors into paying customers.
        - Cart Abandonment Rates: Identify at which stage potential customers drop off, helping to refine checkout processes.
        - Average Order Value (AOV): Measure the average revenue generated per order to strategize upselling and cross-selling
    - For a SaaS startup:
        - Monthly Recurring Revenue (MRR): Monitor predictable revenue streams over time.
        - Customer Churn Rate: Assess how many customers leave over a specific period and refine retention strategies.
        - Average Revenue Per User (ARPU): Track the revenue generated per customer to evaluate pricing models.

2. **Choose Your Data Sources**:
    - Identify all relevant data sources such as:
        - Website analytics tools (e.g., Google Analytics).
        - Customer relationship management (CRM) platforms (e.g., Braze, HubSpot, Salesforce).
        - Data warehouses for scalable data management (e.g., Google BigQuery, Snowflake, Databricks).
    - Ensure data sources are reliable, up-to-date, and well-integrated with your chosen dashboard tool.

3. **Prepare Your Data**:
   - Create a dedicated dataset in your data warehouse (e.g., BigQuery, Snowflake, Databricks) named "Reporting" to centralize metrics.
     - This dataset should include pre-aggregated metrics such as acquisition, retention, and engagement, calculated at daily, weekly, and monthly intervals.
     - Perform transformations to ensure metrics are clean, consistent, and ready for direct use in dashboards.
     - By pre-calculating metrics, you reduce the load on visualization tools, ensuring faster performance.
   - Clean and standardize the data to ensure accuracy and consistency. Steps include:
     - Removing duplicates, filling in missing values, and unifying formats.
     - Validating data quality to avoid misleading insights.
     - Applying additional transformations, such as aggregating or filtering data, to make it ready for visualization.

4. **Import Data into the Visualization Tool**:
   - Connect your visualization tool (e.g., Tableau, Power BI, Google Data Studio) to the prepared data sources.
   - Use connectors or APIs provided by the tool to seamlessly integrate data.
   - Test the connection to ensure that the imported data reflects updates and changes in real time.
   - Validate data mapping to confirm that metrics and dimensions are correctly linked to their visualizations.

5. **Select Visualizations**:
   - Choose the right visualization for the type of data and insights you want to convey:
     - Funnel Charts: Highlight drop-off rates along the customer journey.
     - Bar Charts: Compare categories, such as regional sales performance.
     - Line Charts: Showcase trends over time, like revenue growth or user engagement.
     - Heatmaps: Identify patterns or anomalies in dense datasets, such as customer activity by region.
   - Label visualizations clearly and avoid unnecessary design elements that distract from the data.

6. **Design for Accessibility**:
   - Simplify navigation by grouping related metrics into sections or tabs. For example:
     - Group customer insights in one section and operational data in another.
   - Use clear headings, intuitive layouts, and color-coding to improve readability.
   - Make dashboards accessible on all devices (desktop, tablet, and mobile).

7. **Test and Iterate**:
   - Gather feedback from key stakeholders to ensure the dashboard meets their needs.
   - Test the usability of filters, drill-down options, and navigation.
   - Continuously update and refine dashboards based on evolving business requirements.

8. **Creating a Self-Serve Tool**:
   - Design dashboards and reporting tools that allow non-technical users to explore data and generate their own reports. This democratizes access to insights and fosters a data-driven culture across the organization.
   - **Key Features**:
     - **Interactive Filters and Drill-Down Capabilities**: Let users explore data subsets, such as filtering by region or product line.
     - **Pre-Built Templates**: Simplify the creation of common reports, reducing setup time.
     - **Drag-and-Drop Interfaces**: Allow non-technical users to customize visualizations with ease.
   - **Implementation Tips**:
     - Use tools like Looker, Tableau, or Google Data Studio that support self-serve features.
     - Conduct training sessions to familiarize teams with the tools.
     - Ensure data access is secure with appropriate user permissions.

By following this step-by-step approach, you can create dashboards that provide clarity, foster collaboration, and empower your organization to make informed, data-driven decisions.ns based on data.

4.5 Automating Reports

Manual reporting can be time-intensive, error-prone, and unsustainable as a business scales. Automating your reports ensures that stakeholders always have access to timely, accurate, and actionable data, while freeing up valuable time for teams. Below is a step-by-step guide to effectively automate reporting:

1. **Schedule Data Refreshes**:
   - Automate the refresh of data pipelines to ensure the underlying data is always current:
     - Use tools like **Google BigQuery**'s scheduled queries or **Apache Airflow** to set up periodic updates at intervals such as hourly, daily, weekly, or monthly, based on business needs.
     - Ensure that pre-aggregated datasets (e.g., acquisition, retention, engagement) are refreshed automatically and stored in the "Reporting" dataset within your data warehouse.
   - Build dependency workflows so updates occur sequentially, ensuring data consistency across reports.

2. **Real-Time Dashboards**:
   - Enable real-time integration with live data sources for dashboards that require up-to-the-minute updates:
     - Use APIs or direct connectors to data sources like Google Analytics, CRM systems, or data warehouses.
     - Configure real-time streaming services, such as **Google Cloud Pub/Sub** or **Apache Kafka**, to feed dashboards with live data.
   - Clearly label dashboards as "real-time" to differentiate them from those updated on a scheduled basis.

3. **Distribute Reports via Email**:
   - Automate the delivery of key reports to stakeholders via email:
     - Use tools like **Google Data Studio**, **Power BI**, or **Tableau** to generate scheduled email reports with PDFs or links to live dashboards.
     - Segment email recipients based on their roles and reporting needs. For example:
       1. Send daily operational reports to team leads.
       2. Deliver weekly and monthly executive summaries to management.
   - Customize email content with highlights of key changes or insights (e.g., "Sales increased by 15% last week").

4. **Set Alerts and Triggers**:
   - Configure automated alerts to notify stakeholders of critical changes or anomalies in data:
     - Define thresholds for key metrics, such as a drop in conversion rate below 5% or a spike in customer churn.
     - Use integrations like **Slack**, **email**, or SMS to deliver alerts instantly to relevant team members.
     - Prioritize actionable alerts by categorizing them as high, medium, or low urgency.

5. **Automate Data Validation**:
   - Include automated checks within the reporting workflow to validate the accuracy and integrity of the data:
     - Use tools like **Great Expectations** or custom scripts to identify inconsistencies, missing data, or anomalies before reports are generated.
   - Set up notifications to alert the data engineering team if issues are detected, ensuring errors are corrected promptly.

6. **Personalize Reporting for Stakeholders**:
   - Leverage automation tools to customize reports based on the specific needs of different departments:
     - For Marketing: Include metrics on campaign performance, lead conversions, and ROI.
     - For Finance: Emphasize revenue, expenses, and profitability trends.
     - For Customer Support: Highlight response times, resolution rates, and customer satisfaction scores (CSAT).
   - Create dynamic templates that adapt to the recipient's role, delivering only the most relevant data.

7. **Monitor Reporting Processes**:
   - Regularly review the performance and reliability of automated reporting workflows:
     - Track metrics such as report generation times, data refresh success rates, and stakeholder engagement with reports.
     - Incorporate feedback loops where stakeholders can request adjustments or additional insights to improve the reporting process.

Benefits of Automating Reports:

- **Time Savings**: Eliminates repetitive manual tasks, allowing teams to focus on analysis and strategy.
- **Data Consistency**: Reduces the risk of errors in reports and ensures a single source of truth.
- **Faster Decision-Making**: Provides stakeholders with real-time or scheduled insights, enabling quicker responses to business needs.
- **Scalability**: Supports the growing data and reporting demands of a scaling organization without increasing operational overhead.

By automating reporting, organizations can ensure seamless access to reliable data, enhance decision-making processes, and foster a culture of efficiency and accountability.

4.6 Best Practices for Dashboards and Reporting

1. **Keep It Actionable**:
   - Ensure every visualization serves a clear purpose and directly drives decisions or actions.
   - Prioritize metrics that are tied to business objectives and can prompt immediate actions.

2. **Optimize for Performance**:
   - Simplify queries and use pre-aggregated data in your warehouse to reduce dashboard load times and improve responsiveness.
   - Optimize data pipelines to ensure dashboards display results without delays, especially for real-time or operational dashboards.

3. **Validate Your Data**:
   - Regularly audit your data sources, pipelines, and calculations to ensure accuracy and maintain trust in your dashboards.
   - Automate validation checks to identify and fix errors in the underlying datasets before they reach end-users.

4. **Engage Stakeholders**:
   - Involve end-users during the design process to understand their needs and tailor dashboards to their specific goals.
   - Provide training or documentation to empower teams to navigate and interpret dashboards effectively.
   - Regularly collect feedback from stakeholders to improve usability and relevance.

5. **Maintain Visual Clarity**:
    - Avoid clutter by focusing on key metrics and limiting unnecessary elements. Use consistent colors, labels, and fonts for a polished design.
    - Leverage whitespace effectively to separate sections and ensure readability.
        - Use a consistent visual hierarchy to highlight the most important insights.

6. **Set Reporting Cadence**:
    - Schedule updates for dashboards based on their intended purpose:
        - Real-time updates for operational metrics.
        - Daily updates for team-level performance tracking.
        - Weekly or monthly updates for strategic reviews and trend analysis.
    - Clearly indicate the refresh frequency on each dashboard to set user expectations.

7. **Implement Data Governance**:
    - Use proper access controls to ensure sensitive data is only available to authorized users, and follow compliance standards like GDPR.
    - Maintain a clear data lineage, so users understand where the data comes from and how it is processed.
    - Educate users about data privacy and security best practices to ensure compliance across the organization.

By following these best practices, your dashboards will not only provide actionable insights but also foster a culture of data-driven decision-making throughout your organization.

4.7 Conclusion

Dashboards and reporting tools are indispensable for startups seeking to unlock the true potential of their data. They empower organizations by simplifying complex datasets into actionable insights, aligning teams around shared objectives, and enabling informed decision-making at every level.

By integrating self-serve tools, dashboards become accessible to all stakeholders, reducing reliance on technical teams while fostering a data-driven culture. Automated reports and refresh schedules ensure that data remains current and relevant, while pre-aggregated datasets optimize performance, allowing dashboards to handle complex metrics seamlessly. Additionally, dashboards act as a unified source of truth, driving collaboration across departments and ensuring that all teams—from marketing to finance—can make decisions based on consistent and accurate data.

Looking ahead, a robust dashboarding strategy lays the foundation for advanced analytics capabilities, such as predictive and prescriptive techniques, enabling startups to scale efficiently while adapting to new challenges. By iterating and refining dashboards through user feedback and evolving needs, startups can ensure their tools remain effective and impactful.

As we move into the next chapter, **Introduction to Data Analytics**, we will explore how descriptive, diagnostic, and predictive analytics can provide deeper insights and help organizations extract even greater value from their data.

Chapter Five: Introduction to Data Analytics

Chapter Five: Introduction to Data Analytics

Data analytics is at the core of deriving value from the vast amounts of data generated by businesses today. It provides the methodologies and tools needed to interpret data, extract meaningful insights, and make informed decisions. This chapter introduces the foundational concepts of data analytics and explores its applications for startups aiming to grow and remain competitive in a data-driven world.

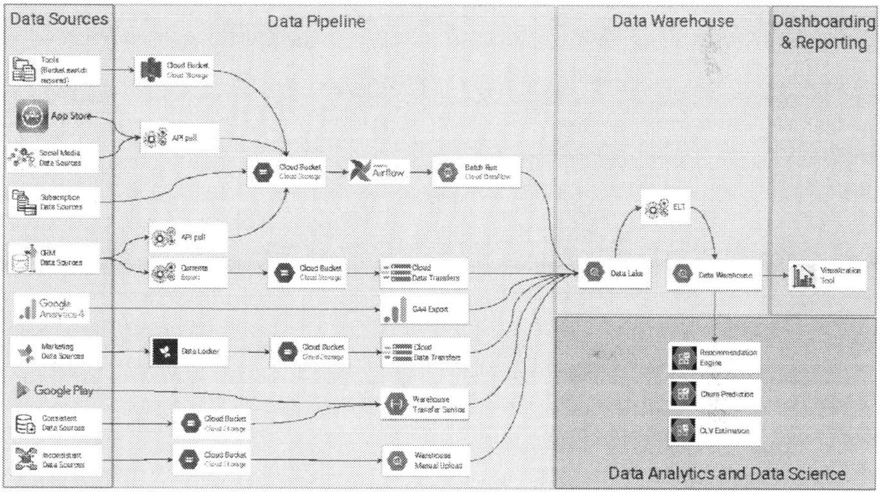

5.1 Fundamentals of Data Analytics

Data analytics is the systematic process of examining raw data to extract actionable insights, identify patterns, and drive better decision-making. It combines statistical techniques, computational tools, and business acumen to turn data into a valuable organizational asset. Startups can harness data analytics to understand their customers, improve operations, and strategize for the future.

At its core, data analytics answers three essential questions:

1. What happened? (Descriptive analytics)
2. Why did it happen? (Diagnostic analytics)
3. What will happen next? (Predictive analytics)

While these are the core questions, a fourth approach, prescriptive analytics, helps businesses decide the best course of action based on predictions and insights. Below are the four primary types of analytics in detail:

1. **Descriptive Analytics**:
   - Descriptive analytics focuses on summarizing historical data to understand past events and trends.
   - It provides a clear picture of what has happened over a specific period and highlights key metrics such as total revenue, user engagement, or website traffic.
   - Example: Calculating Customer Lifetime Value (CLV) to measure how much revenue a customer generates over their engagement with your business.

2. **Diagnostic Analytics**:
   - Diagnostic analytics delves deeper into data to uncover the reasons behind specific outcomes.
   - By identifying trends, anomalies, and root causes, this type of analysis enables organizations to address issues and refine strategies.
   - Example: Analyzing churn rate to understand why customers are leaving your platform and identifying patterns that contribute to churn.

3. **Predictive Analytics**:
   - Predictive analytics uses historical data, statistical algorithms, and machine learning to forecast future outcomes.
   - It helps businesses anticipate trends, mitigate risks, and make proactive decisions.
   - Example: Using a recommendation engine to predict customer preferences and personalize their experience.
   - For startups, leveraging third-party tools such as Google Cloud AI or AWS Machine Learning is a cost-effective way to implement predictive analytics without building complex models in-house.

4. **Prescriptive Analytics**:
   - Prescriptive analytics goes one step further by recommending specific actions based on data insights and predictions.
   - It enables businesses to optimize operations, allocate resources effectively, and make data-backed decisions.
   - Example: Adjusting pricing strategies based on predictive models to maximize profit margins or suggesting product bundling strategies.

Together, these analytics types form the foundation of a comprehensive data strategy, enabling startups to transform raw data into meaningful insights and actionable plans.

5.2 The Role of Data Analytics

Data analytics plays a pivotal role in enabling organizations to leverage data effectively for strategic and operational benefits. Regardless of size or industry, businesses can harness analytics to make data-driven decisions, optimize processes, and gain a competitive edge. Here are the key ways data analytics contributes to organizational success:

- **Enhanced Decision-Making**: By providing evidence-based insights, analytics reduces reliance on intuition and ensures that decisions are grounded in data. Whether forecasting market trends or optimizing resource allocation, data analytics empowers organizations to act with confidence.
- **Customer Insights**: Analyzing customer data enables businesses to understand preferences, behaviors, and pain points. This facilitates personalized experiences, targeted marketing, and improved customer satisfaction, driving loyalty and retention.
- **Operational Efficiency**: Data analytics identifies inefficiencies in workflows, supply chains, and resource allocation. By pinpointing areas for improvement, organizations can streamline operations and reduce costs.
- **Risk Management**: Analytics tools help predict potential risks and mitigate them proactively. For instance, identifying fraud patterns or anticipating market downturns enables businesses to implement preventive measures.
- **Market Competitiveness**: Staying ahead of competitors requires understanding market trends, consumer demands, and emerging opportunities. Data analytics allows organizations to adapt strategies in real-time, ensuring they remain agile and responsive.
- **Innovation and Growth**: By uncovering new opportunities through data, businesses can innovate product offerings, explore untapped markets, and develop strategies to scale effectively.

In today's data-rich environment, organizations that prioritize analytics are better positioned to navigate uncertainties, achieve operational excellence, and capitalize on growth opportunities. By embedding analytics into their decision-making processes, they can drive long-term success and sustainability.

5.3 The Data Analytics Process

The data analytics process is a structured approach that transforms raw data into actionable insights. By following a systematic methodology, organizations can ensure that their analysis is accurate, efficient, and aligned with business goals. Below are the key steps:

1. **Define Objectives**:
   - Clearly articulate the problem or opportunity you want to address through data analytics.
   - Examples include improving customer retention, optimizing product pricing, or identifying operational inefficiencies.
   - Well-defined objectives align the analytics process with business strategies and help focus efforts on actionable outcomes.
2. **Collect Data**:
   - Gather relevant data from internal and external sources, such as CRM systems, website analytics tools, transactional databases, or third-party APIs.
   - Ensure the data is representative and reliable to accurately reflect the business processes under analysis.
   - For instance, an e-commerce company might collect data from sales transactions, customer interactions, and website traffic logs.
3. **Clean and Prepare Data**:
   - Address issues such as missing values, duplicate records, and inconsistent formats to ensure data quality.
   - Data preparation may include creating new metrics, aggregating data for summaries, or standardizing formats for consistency.
   - This step minimizes errors and ensures the data is ready for analysis.
4. **Analyze Data**:
   - Apply statistical techniques, machine learning, or exploratory methods to uncover trends, correlations, and anomalies.

- Tools such as Python, R, SQL, or visualization platforms like Looker, Tableau or Power BI can support this stage.
- Techniques may include clustering for customer segmentation, regression for sales forecasting, or sentiment analysis for customer feedback.

5. **Interpret Results**:
    - Translate analytical findings into insights that stakeholders can understand and act upon.
    - Use reports, dashboards, and visualizations to present the data
    - Example: A marketing team might use segmentation analysis to craft targeted campaigns for high-value customers.

6. **Take Action**:
    - Implement strategies and initiatives informed by the analytics insights.
    - Monitor outcomes to assess the impact of these actions and adjust approaches as necessary.
    - For instance, addressing high churn rates revealed by diagnostics might involve redesigning the onboarding experience.

7. **Automate and Iterate**:
    - Automate repetitive tasks such as data collection, transformation, and reporting to improve efficiency and scalability.
    - Revisit and refine the analytics process regularly, incorporating new data, technologies, and feedback to stay aligned with evolving objectives.

By following these steps, organizations can establish a reliable analytics framework that consistently delivers actionable insights, enabling data-driven decisions and long-term success.

5.4 Challenges in Data Analytics

While data analytics offers immense benefits, organizations often face challenges that can hinder their ability to fully leverage its potential. Addressing these challenges is essential for creating a robust and sustainable analytics framework. Below are some of the common challenges in data analytics:

1. **Data Quality Issues**:
   - Poor-quality data, such as incomplete, inconsistent, or outdated information, can lead to inaccurate conclusions and flawed decisions.
   - Example: A retail company analyzing sales trends might overestimate demand due to duplicate records or missing product returns data.
   - **Solution**: Implement data validation and cleaning processes, and establish frameworks to maintain data integrity.
2. **Lack of Expertise**:
   - Organizations may lack the in-house skills to manage, analyze, and interpret complex datasets, particularly in areas like machine learning and advanced analytics.
   - Example: A startup with a few resources may struggle to build predictive models or optimize analytics workflows.
   - **Solution**: Invest in training, hire skilled professionals, or partner with third-party analytics providers to bridge the expertise gap.
3. **Scalability**:
   - As businesses grow, the volume, variety, and velocity of data increase, necessitating scalable infrastructure and processes.
   - Example: An e-commerce platform experiencing rapid growth may encounter slower query times or storage limitations in legacy systems.
   - **Solution**: Adopt cloud-native solutions like BigQuery etc, which offer elastic scaling and support for large datasets.

4. **Privacy and Compliance**:
   - Organizations handling sensitive customer data must navigate complex regulations such as GDPR, CCPA etc.
   - Example: A healthcare provider failing to anonymize patient data risks legal penalties and reputational damage.
   - **Solution**: Implement robust data security measures, anonymize sensitive information, and stay updated on regulatory requirements.

5. **Integration Challenges**:
   - Data is often siloed across multiple systems, making it difficult to consolidate and analyze holistically.
   - Example: A marketing team might struggle to combine social media metrics with CRM data to measure campaign ROI effectively.
   - **Solution**: Use a common identifier to tag a customer, so that you can tag data from diverse sources into a unified platform.

6. **Interpreting Insights**:
   - Even with well-processed data, translating analytics outputs into actionable strategies can be a challenge.
   - Example: A finance team receiving churn predictions might lack clarity on how to address retention gaps effectively.
   - **Solution**: Collaborate across departments to contextualize insights and create clear action plans tied to business objectives.

By recognizing and proactively addressing these challenges, organizations can maximize the value of their data analytics initiatives and ensure long-term success.

5.5 Conclusion

Data analytics stands as the capstone of an organization's journey toward becoming data-driven. Throughout this chapter, we have explored how analytics can transform raw data into actionable insights, empowering businesses to make informed decisions, streamline operations, and adapt to changing market conditions.

By mastering foundational techniques—descriptive, diagnostic, predictive, and prescriptive analytics—organizations can address past challenges, predict future opportunities, and define strategic pathways forward. However, the journey is not without challenges. Data quality issues, integration hurdles, and the complexities of scaling infrastructure are hurdles that must be proactively addressed. These obstacles underline the need for robust processes, skilled teams, and a commitment to continuous improvement.

With a solid foundation in data analytics, the possibilities for exploration and innovation are limitless. The frameworks, tools, and strategies shared throughout this book will serve as your guide to unlocking the transformative power of data for your organization. This is just the beginning—the next chapters in your data journey are yours to write.

Summary

Chapter-Wise Summary

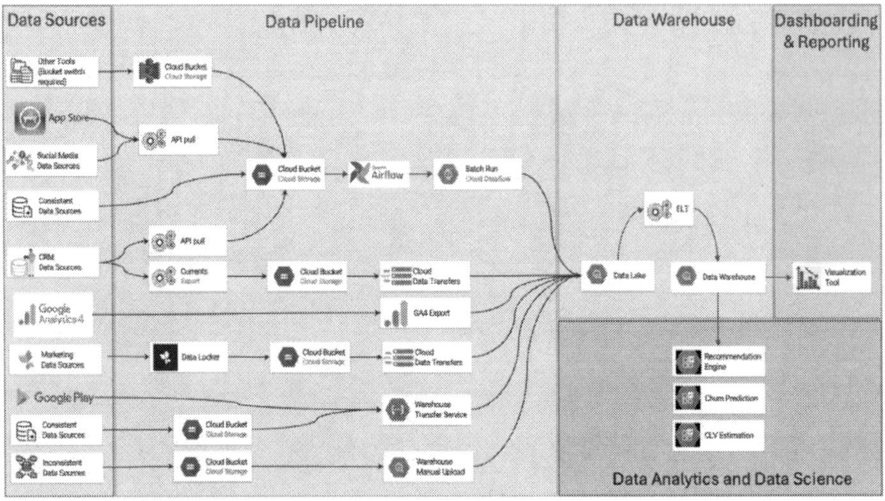

Chapter One: Building the Foundation

This chapter lays the groundwork for creating a robust data strategy in startups. It emphasizes the importance of data in making informed decisions, optimizing operations, and driving business growth. Key focus areas include defining data goals, understanding business-specific metrics, and selecting foundational tools for data collection and organization. The chapter also highlights practical examples and actionable steps for setting up a strong data foundation.

Chapter Two: Building Data Pipelines

This chapter introduces the concept of data pipelines as the nervous system of an organization, enabling the seamless flow of data from source to storage. It explains the difference between batch and real-time processing and provides a step-by-step guide to building efficient pipelines. Topics covered include data extraction, transformation, and loading (ELT), the use of orchestration tools like Apache Airflow and Prefect, and strategies for ensuring data reliability and scalability.

Chapter Three: Data Warehousing

A data warehouse serves as the centralized hub for storing, organizing, and analyzing structured data. This chapter explores the significance of data warehousing in startups, including its role in consolidating disparate data sources and preparing data for analytics. It provides guidance on selecting the right platform (e.g., Google BigQuery, Snowflake), designing schemas, and implementing best practices like incremental loading, partitioning, and clustering to optimize performance.

Chapter Four: Building Dashboards and Reporting

This chapter focuses on transforming raw data into actionable insights through well-designed dashboards and automated reporting tools. It covers principles of dashboard design, such as structuring dashboards by business functions, ensuring clarity, and enabling interactivity. Practical steps for building dashboards include identifying key metrics, preparing data for visualization, and automating reports for real-time decision-making. The chapter also discusses the role of self-serve tools in empowering non-technical teams and fostering a data-driven culture.

Chapter Five: Introduction to Data Analytics

The final chapter introduces the fundamental concepts of data analytics, including descriptive, diagnostic, predictive, and prescriptive analytics. It highlights practical use cases like calculating Customer Lifetime Value (CLV), analyzing churn rates, and leveraging third-party tools for predictive modeling. Challenges such as data quality, scalability, and compliance are addressed, along with strategies to overcome them. The chapter concludes with a call to action for embracing a data-first mindset to drive sustainable growth and innovation.

Epilogue

As this book comes to a close, it marks the beginning of a transformative journey for you and your startup. Building a strong data foundation isn't just about implementing tools and processes—it's about adopting a mindset where data becomes an integral part of decision-making and strategy. The steps outlined in this guide are designed to help you not only navigate the complexities of data but also harness its power to create scalable, impactful, and sustainable growth.

Startups face unique challenges: limited resources, rapidly changing priorities, and the constant need to make critical decisions. By focusing on a structured approach to data, as described in these chapters, you can overcome these hurdles with confidence. From setting up robust data pipelines and warehouses to designing dashboards that empower your team, every step builds on the next to form a cohesive and reliable data ecosystem.

Key takeaways from this book include:

- **The Importance of Starting Strong**: Building a solid data foundation ensures scalability and reliability as startup grows.
- **The Value of Collaboration**: Dashboards, reporting tools, and analytics should not just inform but also unite your team around shared goals and insights.
- **The Journey of Analytics**: From descriptive to predictive analytics, every step enhances your ability to respond to challenges and seize opportunities.

Remember, becoming a data-driven organization doesn't happen overnight. It requires persistence, adaptability, and continuous learning. Embrace the iterative nature of this journey—start simple, experiment, learn from your results, and iterate to refine your approach.

This book provides the foundational knowledge to get you started, but the possibilities of what you can achieve with data are endless. Whether it's launching innovative products, entering new markets, or creating unparalleled customer experiences, your ability to leverage data will determine your competitive edge.

As you move forward, remember: Data is not just a tool—it's the story of your startup's journey. Every metric, insight, and decision reflects the progress you've made and the opportunities that lie ahead. Use this story to inspire, innovate, and grow.

Thank you for allowing me to be part of your data journey. May your business thrive, your data systems evolve, and your insights lead you to extraordinary success.

As this journey of exploring the foundations of data for entrepreneurs comes to an end, I would like to leave you with a thought:

"In a data-driven culture,
the story is written by
the insights and the actions
they inspire."

Appendix

Bibliography

1. **Articles and Reports**
    - Google Cloud. *Best Practices for Building Scalable Data Pipelines.* Google Cloud Blog, 2022.
    - Google Cloud Resources: https://cloud.google.com/free/
    - Snowflake Resources: https://www.snowflake.com/en/resources
    - Tableau Resources: https://www.tableau.com/why-tableau
2. **Tools and Documentation**
    - Google BigQuery Documentation: https://cloud.google.com/bigquery/docs
    - Apache Airflow Documentation: https://airflow.apache.org/
    - Looker Documentation: https://looker.com/
    - Databricks Documentation: https://www.databricks.com/
    - ChatGPT by OpenAI: https://openai.com/chatgpt
3. **Personal Experience**
    - Insights and frameworks derived from personal experience as an entrepreneur and professional in data-driven businesses.

About the Author

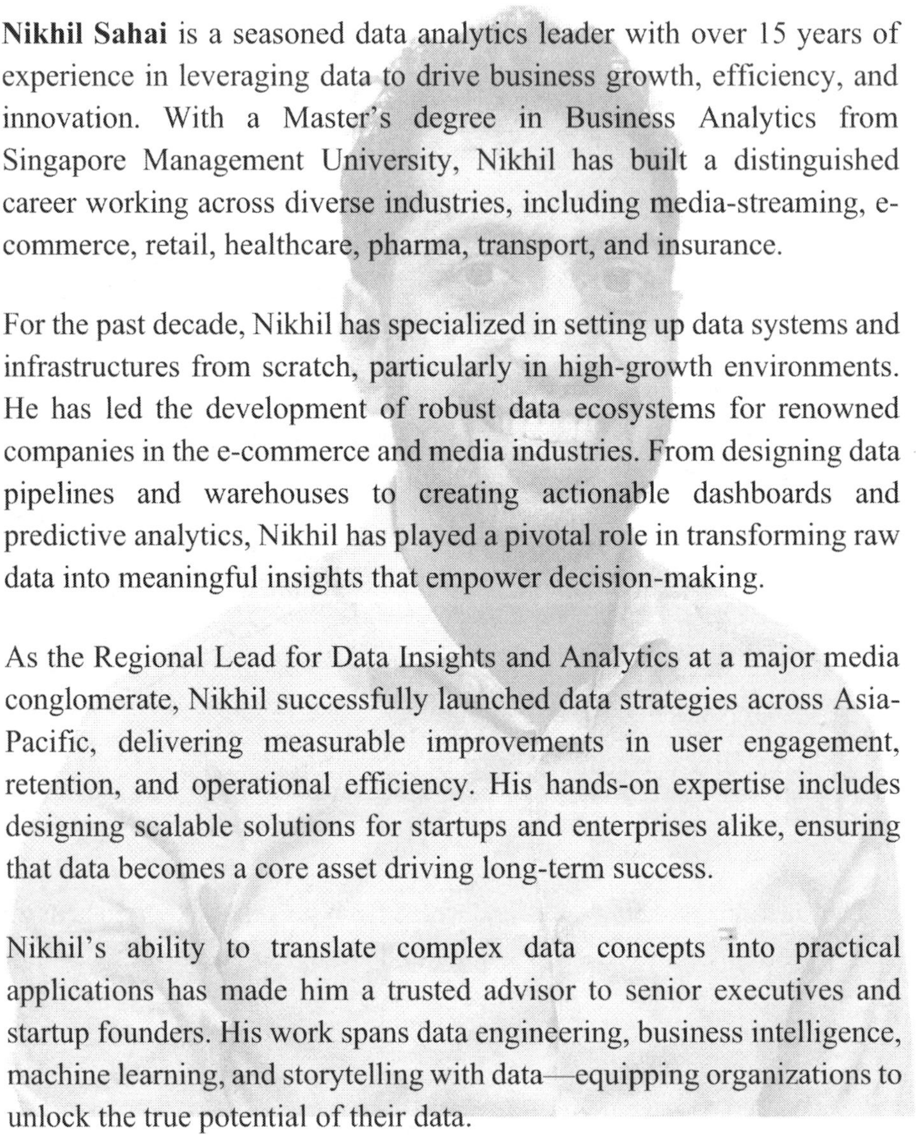

Nikhil Sahai is a seasoned data analytics leader with over 15 years of experience in leveraging data to drive business growth, efficiency, and innovation. With a Master's degree in Business Analytics from Singapore Management University, Nikhil has built a distinguished career working across diverse industries, including media-streaming, e-commerce, retail, healthcare, pharma, transport, and insurance.

For the past decade, Nikhil has specialized in setting up data systems and infrastructures from scratch, particularly in high-growth environments. He has led the development of robust data ecosystems for renowned companies in the e-commerce and media industries. From designing data pipelines and warehouses to creating actionable dashboards and predictive analytics, Nikhil has played a pivotal role in transforming raw data into meaningful insights that empower decision-making.

As the Regional Lead for Data Insights and Analytics at a major media conglomerate, Nikhil successfully launched data strategies across Asia-Pacific, delivering measurable improvements in user engagement, retention, and operational efficiency. His hands-on expertise includes designing scalable solutions for startups and enterprises alike, ensuring that data becomes a core asset driving long-term success.

Nikhil's ability to translate complex data concepts into practical applications has made him a trusted advisor to senior executives and startup founders. His work spans data engineering, business intelligence, machine learning, and storytelling with data—equipping organizations to unlock the true potential of their data.

An accomplished public speaker, Nikhil has shared his insights on data management and analytics at several high-profile industry conferences. His innovative contributions have earned him numerous accolades, including performance awards for delivering impactful, data-backed results.

When he's not solving data challenges, Nikhil shares his knowledge through blogs on his website, experiments with emerging technologies like home automation, and participates in marathons, triathlons, and mountain trekking. He believes that data is not just about numbers—it's a narrative that every business needs to craft for its growth.

In *Data for Entrepreneurs: Basic Data Setup Guide*, Nikhil combines his wealth of experience and passion for data to guide startup founders, tech leads, and business managers in building strong data foundations. With this book, he demystifies the process of setting up data infrastructure, offering practical strategies and actionable advice to empower young companies to thrive in today's data-driven world.

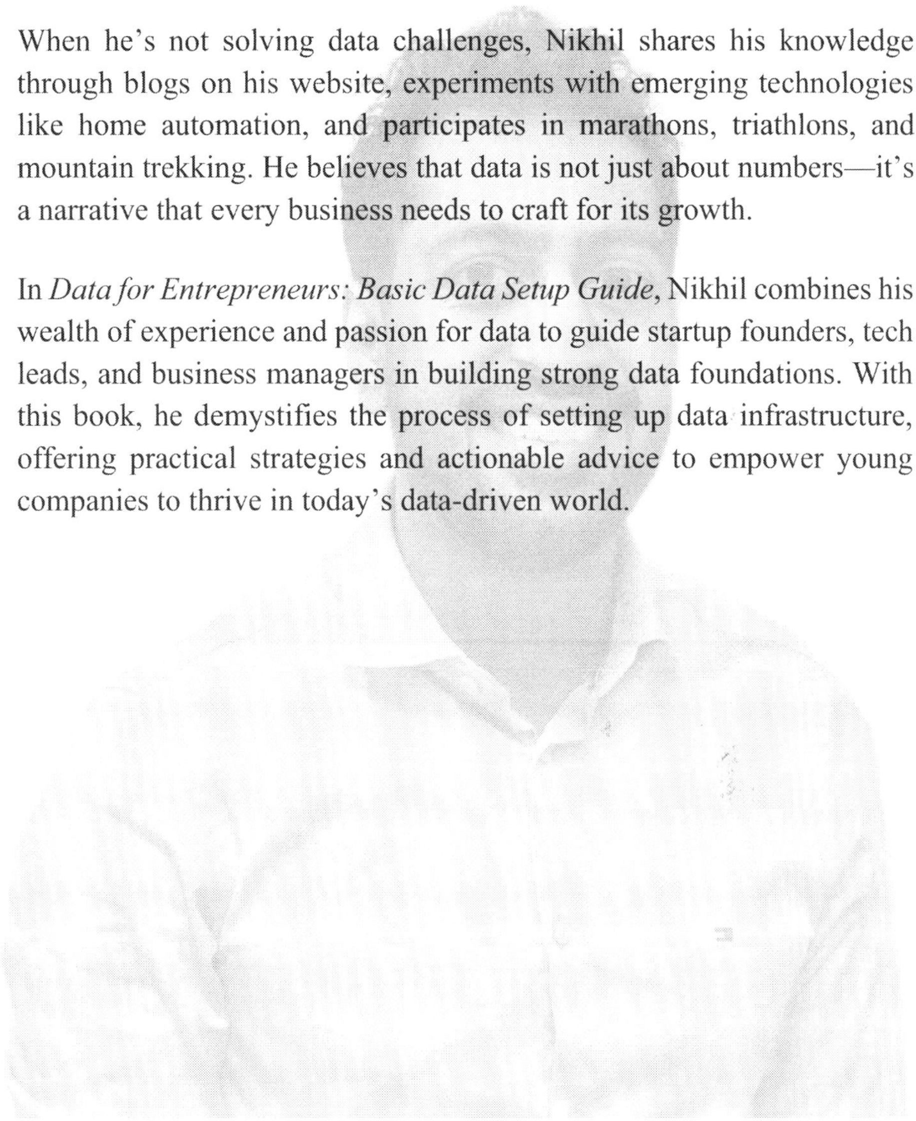

Notes

Notes

Notes

Made in the USA
Monee, IL
07 March 2025

1dc3b66d-8bb5-493b-b4f9-713f20b830b0R01